T0146583

PARADIGMS *of* MARRIAGE
WORKBOOK

PARADIGMS *of* MARRIAGE
WORKBOOK

Dr. Robert O. A. Samms, PhD.

Dr. Pamela R. Samms, DEd.

iUniverse

PARADIGMS OF MARRIAGE WORKBOOK

iUniverse books may be ordered through booksellers or by contacting:

iUniverse
1663 Liberty Drive
Bloomington, IN 47403
www.iuniverse.com
1-800-Authors (1-800-288-4677)

ISBN: 978-1-5320-3398-8 (sc)
ISBN: 978-1-5320-3399-5 (e)

Print information available on the last page.

iUniverse rev. date: 02/09/2018

Foreword

It is a privilege and honour for me to participate in the writing of this workbook.

Dr. Pamela Samms was a great woman of integrity, virtue, class, prudence, love, spirituality, and patience. She was my dearest friend, confidante, and mentor. Her quiet strength and profound guidance helped me through many rocky days and nights of struggle, confusion, and panic as an abandoned wife and single mother.

I honour, praise, and thank Almighty God for giving me the opportunity to follow Sister Pamela's work alongside the sweetheart of her youth, Dr. Robert Samms. Marriage Motivational Series is advancing the work God called us to do—educating couples, healing, growing relationships, and leading families to Christ. Thank you my dearest friend, Sister Pamela, for your prudence and guidance. I dearly miss you and our private talks, but by the Grace of our Loving God I will greet you in His Kingdom.

Thank you, Robert, for your love, support, strength, patience, wisdom, guidance, and encouragement. May many families be blessed and healed through our ministry as we all work and await the soon coming of our Lord and Saviour Jesus Christ.

To Sister Pamela's four children, spouses, and twelve grandchildren:

I know you love and miss your mother and grandnan immensely. By God's grace, I will honour her memory and life's work, and love and support your dad and grandpoppy.

To my daughter:

You are my precious miracle and gift. I love you very much and thank God for giving you to me.

To all my family, extended family, and dear friends:

Your prayers, love, support, and encouragement inspired me. I love you and thank you.

To All the individuals and families who may find this workbook:

Pay strict attention to its messages and strategies in order to heal and grow your life, your marriage, and your family. Please share these pages with others.

Dearest Heavenly Father, please anoint, bless, guide, empower and protect your man-servant, Pastor Robert Samms, and me as we advance the mission You called and commissioned us. We endeavor to walk in the footsteps of Jesus (Luke 4:18,19) as we seek to bless individuals and families. Thank You for answering my prayer through the name of Your son, Jesus Christ.

Couples, be strong and courageous and use the principles in this workbook to improve your love life, grow passionate relationship, and build happy families.

Your Humble Servant.

Petula Samms

Dedication

This workbook is dedicated posthumously to Dr. Pamela Samms who used her skills as a teacher for more than forty years and her training as Marriage Educator to create and organize the activities for this workbook. She was devoted to completing her assignment for this workbook until a brief illness led to her unexpected death.

We also dedicate this workbook to Edmond Harris Theophilus Dow, the likely last of twelve Drs. Samms' grandchildren. Little Edmond was their only grandchild born after Dr. Pamela Samms passing.

We further dedicate this workbook to the many couples who, recognizing their need for growth in their marriage, use its rich resources in collaboration with *Paradigms of Marriage* to their best advantage.

It is our hope that countless number of couples worldwide will benefit richly from the seminars conducted by Dr. Robert and Petula Samms as this new phase of the Marriage Motivational Series is launched.

Purpose

The purpose of this workbook is to provide practical exercises for attendees to the Marriage Motivational Series seminars and those desiring to devote personal study time to improve their understanding of marriage/family relationships. The workbook is based on a chapter by chapter review of the book *Paradigms of Marriage* **by Dr. Robert Samms.** In this workbook, Dr. Samms has used the opportunity to add updates to his original publication of *Paradigms of Marriage*.

The seminar series consist of ten presentations. Each of the ten presentations requires about two hours, including time for modeling and participation activities. The Ten Paradigm series are suited for religious and non-religious couples and groups. It is grounded in the concept that the Bible contains the fundamental principles for successful relationships as well as human conduct. However, we collaborate with scientific research findings to achieve the best possible outcome, especially as connection is made with current everyday situations. The delivery of this series in our ten seminars considers the type of audience, whether religious or non-religious. The companion family seminar series called Family & Faith (ten presentations based on the book *Family & Faith*, authored by Drs. Robert & Pamela Samms) is based directly on the principles of Scripture. In the book *Family & Faith*, the authors draw relevant lessons from selected Biblical families and teachings to assist contemporary families in their arduous task of building successful family relationships. During the seminars, Dr. Robert and Petula Samms will draw on their own experiences as well as training to enrich their presentations.

Considering the incredibly high divorce rate in North America (nearly 50%) and the alarming breakdown of family relationships, it is our hope that these series will assist in helping couples before they embark on their marital journey as well as couples in conflict, difficult parent and children challenges, and those successful couples or families in harmony but seeking for strategies to grow their relationships with spouse and children.

As attendees at the seminars listen to and participate in the presentations and exercises, they will be able to select the issues that apply best to their situation and record them for future reflection. Participation activities focus on specific issues that couples need to sort out and share with each other. The participation level of each person will be self-determined. No attempt will be made to impose any requirement for public participation. In other words, participation will be voluntary. For best results, however, we encourage full group participation.

The exercises in this workbook will be closely linked to the resource book, ***Paradigms of Marriage***. Each chapter will follow with appropriate exercises. It is necessary to read the corresponding chapter in *Paradigms of Marriage* for background information. Give special attention to the paradigm for that chapter. It presents a cryptic pattern containing the main concept that provides the key for a better understanding of the chapter.

The main concept on which the entire paradigm series pivot is:

Marriage Provides Happiness but Skills are Needed.

Aristotle informs us that happiness is the meaning and purpose of life. It is the whole aim and end of our existence. **Happiness is the only thing we attain as an end in itself. Everything else we do is toward achieving happiness**. When the partner delivers the expected support for happiness of the spouse, the marriage moves toward "Paradise" but when the partner fails to deliver, the marriage moves inexorably toward the proverbial "Pit".

In this world, we experience problems, pain, and death. To those who accept and obey God's commandments, Jesus offers salvation--unlimited happiness with eternal life-when He returns and sets up His Kingdom (See Revelation chapter 21). However, in this temporal existence, our best path to happiness may be experienced within marriage and family. Marriage and family are God's most precious gifts to us apart from our connection with Him and life itself. It is given to us for our happiness and to perpetuate the name of God in the earth (See Deuteronomy chapter 6: 5-9). That is the reason marriage is sacred. Sex is the sacred gift that binds marriage. Any attempt to change marriage as God ordained it or corrupt it by sexual activities outside the marital union is condemned before God (See: Matthew 19: 9; Exodus 20: 14; Ephesians 5: 29-33; I Corinthians 6: 18-20).

God employs the sanctity of marriage as a metaphor to describe the relationship between Christ and the Church. We have the option of using our God-given gift of freedom of choice to accept or reject God's laws that clearly reveal how we should live. No one should be prevented from making this personal choice because our decision has serious eternal consequences. Although we have a duty as Christians to present Biblical truth in order that others may honor God's requirements, we should love everyone regardless of his/her choices. Only God condemns: our duty is to love all people as Jesus certainly did and the Bible enjoins. **Regardless of our dislike of certain behaviors, we should exercise love, understanding, and tolerant for everyone.**

The authors hope that many couples and individuals who read and do the exercises in this workbook, read carefully *Paradigms of Marriage*, and *Family & Faith* as well as attend the seminars will receive invaluable insights as they seek true happiness in this life and eternal happiness in the life to come.

About the Authors

Greetings! This is to introduce Marriage Motivational Series, Family & Faith Series, and Marriage Enrichment Events as well as information about the authors, who are Marriage Educators.

This project was born in the Spring of 2001. While listening to the news, Dr. Robert Samms heard again the alarming divorce statistics. In the United States, the divorce rate between 1965 and 1980 doubled. The rate in Canada was not significantly different. Recent statistics reveal that nearly five out of every ten marriages may end in divorce and another thirty to forty percent may likely be experiencing troubled relationships but remain together for various reasons. Until her passing in February, 2012, Dr. Pamela Samms partnered with Dr. Robert Samms to develop the Marriage Motivational Series for assisting married couples to grow successful relationships.

After marrying again, Dr. Robert Samms and his wife, Petula, decided to dedicate their lives to continue the task of assisting couples and families. We recognize that several marriage educators and counselors render outstanding service to those who seek assistance, but they are too few for the overwhelming task. Dr. Robert and Petula Samms have decided to combine the principles gained from their past and current marriage experiences, buttressed by extensive research and specialized training, to develop the seminar series.

Born in England and brought up in Canada, Petula has brought into their marriage relationship a valuable set of skills and experience. During her many years as a successful single mom (due to divorce beyond her control), she developed several useful skills that may assist others who are enduring similar experiences. Petula is a trained vocalist and certified Marriage Enrichment Facilitator.

Dr. Robert Samms spent several years researching, writing, and publishing *Making Marriage Meaningful: Insights and Secrets from a 40-Year Marriage* that presents fourteen facets of marriage. They represent some of the key aspects (negative and positive) that emerged after a keen analysis of the forty years of marriage between Dr. Samms and his former wife, Dr. Pamela Samms. He researched each topic to discover key concepts and successful strategies employed by leading marriage therapists, marriage counselors, and other marriage professionals and authors. Understandably, he drew on his four plus decades of pastoral marriage and family counseling, duties as a marriage officer, Pastor, Superintendent of Education, and President of the Quebec Conference of Seventh-day Adventist Churches in Canada. His life's experience also includes living and working in four countries: Jamaica, Bahamas, Canada, and the United States. The other publication, *Paradigms of Marriage*, parallels the PowerPoint presentations for the marriage education series. The presentations cover ten key areas of marriage. The newer series, *Family & Faith,* **is a ten-part Biblically based family series. The two ten-part seminar series are based on the books,** *Family & Faith* **and** *Paradigms of Marriage* **separately. The books are available through any major book store, online, directly** from the author or iUniverse Publishing Inc. More information may be available at the website: FamilyMarriageConsulting.com or Facebook page (Facebook.com/DrRobertSamms).

The purpose of our presentations is to reveal some of the key causes for the failure of so many marriages and offer helpful strategies to promote successful marriages. Fortunately, iUniverse Publishing has designated *Making Marriage Meaningful* "**Editor's Choice**," thereby introducing it to the public with a stamp of professional approval.

As Marriage & Family Educators, Dr. Robert and Petula Samms conduct seminars and private consultations by appointment.

Table of Contents

Introduction

BEGINNING

Since 2001, Drs. Robert and Pamela Samms, and more recently Petula Samms, have been planning and developing a program to assist married and unmarried couples as well as families. Pam had spent more than forty years in the field of education and Robert spent about forty-eight years in disciplines related to human relationships with most of that time spent as administrator and minister, with strong emphasis on pastoral marriage and family counseling. But the time had come for more serious preparation to launch an assault on marital breakdowns and aid couples and families to move from devastating painful conflicts to exhilarating pleasurable experiences. But how?

As I considered the divorce rate that settled between forty-eight and fifty-two percent from the late seventies to the present, I knew the task would be difficult but not insuperable. What was more, the society, including the clergy and the various levels of government, seemed to be more focused on the alarming problems in the society that resulted from broken and problematic families than on the obvious solution—**Marriage Education!** The effort focused more on curative rather than preventive strategies. I discovered the dire need for marriage and family education during the five-year research and preparation.

HISTORY

In the early 1960s, three religious men, a Roman Catholic priest, Father Gabriel Calvo, in Spain; Minister Leon Smith, a United Methodist Church minister, and his wife Antoinette, and Dr. David Mace, a Quaker (marriage counselor/sociologist) and his wife, Vera, in the United States, recognized that marriage was being transformed from the traditional/hierarchical pattern to a very different model that is now known as Companionship Marriage or Partnership Marriage. This new approach to relationships was destined to transform marriage and families. It required education to cope successfully with its demands in this new form of relationship dynamic. They began developing programs to assist couples to adapt to this new marriage model. Their approaches were different but their attempts were notably creative concepts.

Dr. Ernest Burgess, a pioneer family sociologist, and a few others observed the impending change from the traditional marriage model and sounded the alarm in the two previous decades. But their concerns were mainly overlooked. What is remarkable is that these three men and two women rose to the challenge of designing programs to assist couples develop coping strategies long before the emergence of a public recognition that there was a need.

Father Calvo introduced Marriage Encounter; The Smiths developed Communication Labs, a program emphasizing marriage education, dialogue, and communication skills, and The Mace's started a program known as Marriage Enrichment that emphasized a special technigue called

Dialogue. Today, this program is well established as Better Marriages, Inc. All of these programs are being used in various forms in different parts of the world to assist couples.

Here is an excerpt from Better Marriages website:

> In the 1940s and 1950s those in the helping professions began to view persons not just as individuals but as people living in family systems. Another contributing factor to what is now called "marriage enrichment" was the shift from "intervention to prevention." This change emphasized the importance of dealing with personal and interpersonal challenges by providing skills and experiential learning for individuals and families before they get into serious difficulty. (History of Better Marriages, Bettermarriages.org).

MARRIAGE EDUCATION VITAL

As mentioned above, one of those men who saw the emerging marriage and family crisis and sought to do something about it was Dr. David Mace. With his wife, Vera, they developed a program for couples called the Marriage Enrichment. Their program developed into a strong organization known today as Better Marriages Inc. Their method is being used widely in many parts of the world. Dr. Mace believed that couples needed education and strategies to deal with the modern companionship or partnership marriage model. Under the previous system that was dominant for millennia until the early nineteen sixties, couples based their marriage relationship on a hierarchical pattern—father, mother, and children—firmly in that order. Therefore, each family member understood his/her role and usually performed it. This system provided more stability to the family as well as the society. The order and respect for authority it provided allowed for less flexibility and more discipline and respect. Children were less inclined to engage in promiscuous sex, become parents prematurely or have abortions and get involved in destructive or abhorrent behaviors, such as social drugs. Husband and wife were less likely to engage in conflicts leading to divorce because the man (husband/father) had the last word when disagreements occurred. Mother ruled the household and father provided the spiritual, and moral leadership for the family.

NEW MARRIAGE MODEL: EGALITARIAN

Not so when this new system emerged in the late nineteen sixties. The hierarchical order was disrupted. An egalitarian system developed and replaced it across the North American society. Not only did the roles husband and wife (father and mother) change radically but the role of the children changed as well. Unable to cope with the result of the disruptive changes the new system brought, combined with other radical social influences within the society, such as the women's movement and the rebellion against authority, divorces increased by more than one hundred percent (100%) within fifteen years.

Alarmed by this outcome, leading voices from those who failed to understand the profound change in marriage model started to proclaim the doom of marriage in our society. In 1989, for instance, Newsweek magazine devoted an entire special issue to proclaim the death of traditional marriage. Others contemplated the possibility of the dissolution of marriage itself. It proclaimed that marriage would be replaced with various forms of relationships. However, we are well into the twenty-first century and family and marriage are still strongly entrenched within our society. Most parents still look to marriage to provide happiness and stability for their sons and daughters. People were not rejecting marriage, they were having difficulty coping with its transformation and new demands. Admittedly, the form of marriage itself has undergone significant metamorphosis, such as homosexual relationships. But marriage and family relationships are still vital for the success of our modern society.

NEW SYSTEM: NEW STRATEGY

What is becoming clearer is that couples entering a companionship marriage relationship with its two-vote system must either have needed skills in negotiation or submit to some form of ongoing marriage education in order to develop helpful marital strategies. The age of the traditional hierarchical pattern of marriage and family relationships with its one-vote system had given way to a more complex pattern. Skills are needed to navigate this current pattern of marriage.

> A marriage that is a one-vote system is largely conflict-free. ---Switch to a two-vote system, however, and you have a situation vastly more difficult to manage. Two conflicting wills mean the possibility of endless disagreement and strife, and if the two persons concerned have plenty of basic differences in their needs and wishes, a state of chronic acerbity is introduced into the relationship. In other words, demand equality in marriage and you take the risk of all hell breaking loose. Unless the couple have highly developed skills in the very complex art of negotiating disagreements, their relationship may soon be in serious trouble. ---
>
> The demand for love and equality turned a relationship that was relatively easy to handle into a very difficult task requiring much more skill than the average couple possessed. It was like getting off a cart horse and mounting a race horse. (Dr. David Mace, *Close Companions*, Winston-Salem, NC: The Association for Couples in Marriage Enrichment, 1982, pp.18,19.)

Ten Paradigms of Marriage series, Family & Faith series, and Marriage Enrichment Group (MEG) are used as marriage education tools to assist married couples and families to develop appropriate strategies and skills to enjoy happy and successful relationships. Although hard work is required to accomplish most tasks or reach any worthwhile goal, we try to make this learning experience a pleasant and enjoyable one.

PARADIGMS OF MARRIAGE VERSUS RECENT RESEARCH

Occasionally, the author of *Paradigms of Marriage* would check with current research to discover whether new scientific findings render marriage analysis and strategies stated in his books were outdated or in need of revision. To date, no reason was found to make any notable changes. One explanation might be that the principles recorded in Dr. Robert Samms publications were based on findings after the changes from the traditional marriage to the current marriage pattern took place. That means, the author experienced and studied the patterns of the two systems after enough changes had occurred in both. We must bear in mind that human beings have the same basic emotions and expectations, regardless of the era in which they live. Cultural systems may shape the behaviors of couples, individuals, and groups but people are people, carrying the same basic needs based on their heredity. Think, for instance, about people living two thousand years ago: Did they have the need for survival, freedom, love and belonging, power, and enjoyment? So do we today! These are built-in needs for all humans and maybe other living beings too. As we have pointed out in this workbook, the traditional system had a set of principles that regulated that system for millennia and the new partnership pattern needs different strategies to produce successful outcomes. The bottom line is that our stated strategies will apply until the current marriage model changes. However, scientific research and statistics may give us a clearer understanding of how we function within the marital system. We may also keep up-to-date through our seminars and Website.

A FEW CURRENT FINDINGS TO BEAR IN MIND

Based on a Pew study of the US Census Bureau information, in 1960, 72 percent of the adult population of the US was married. In 2011, it collapsed to 51 percent. Men and women are marrying later. Ages changed from early twenties to mid and late twenties. Compared to 1960s when statistically few women were living with a partner before marriage, currently more than 10 percent of women are living with a partner outside of marriage. Between 1995 and 2010, women married before age 25 dropped by about 15 percent (See: Anna Miller, "The Changing Face---and age---of Marriage", Monitor On Psychology, April, 2013.).

STRESS: THE MODERN MARITAL ENEMY

One recent study showed a factor that has become evident in causing marital problems. It is certainly a modern contribution to the complexity of life couples must face as contrasted with previous generations under the traditional pattern of marriages. In an article, Anna Miller points to evidence that stress is a major factor for modern marriages.

> In one 2012 study, graduate student April Buck, PhD, and social psychologist Lisa Neff, PhD, from the University of Texas at Austin, evaluated diaries of 165 newlywed couples. Every day for 14 days, each participant responded to prompts about stressful circumstances (such as getting stuck in traffic), the energy expended to handle those stressors, their positive and negative interactions with partners, and their levels of satisfaction with their relationships.

> Not surprisingly, the researchers found that on the most stressful days, spouses reported more negative behaviors toward their partners and less satisfaction with their relationships. The psychologists posit that the energy dedicated toward handling stressful events detracts from the energy needed to maintain a good relationship (*Journal of Family Psychology*, 2012).

It would be easy to conclude that marital stress mainly affects those in the lower economic classes or those with lower education but the studies reveal that all groups within the society are affected. The research reveals that the effect of stress on the lower income group had less resiliency because they had less resources to deal with the problems when they occur. For instance, if a couple has little or no money in the bank and no credit card when the car breaks down on their way to work, the impact of the stress would be magnified in contrast to someone who could just call for service for the car while he/she takes a taxi to work. The poor couple would experience additional relationship issues while struggling with the problems.

> Couples who rarely get a chance to restore their "reserves," such as those from low-income communities, can be particularly prone to marital dissatisfaction and divorce. In one study using data from about 4,500 respondents to the Florida Family Formation Survey, social psychologist Benjamin Karney, PhD, of the University of California, Los Angeles, and colleagues found that the marriages of lower-income couples were more likely to be hurt by stressful life events and mental health problems than the marriages of the more affluent couples. (Ibid.)

Yet the more affluent couples still experience stress and must deal with it even though they have more resources. In fact, their lifestyle could create other issues with which they have to cope. With extra funds on hand, they could more likely spend more time with expensive entertainment that keep them apart from each other.

> Analysis of the same data set found that all respondents — regardless of income level — reported similar problems within their relationships, such as wanting more affection and struggling to communicate effectively with their partners. Lower-income groups, however, experienced more problems related to economic and social issues such as drinking or drug abuse (*Journal of Marriage and Family*, 2012) (Anna Miller, "Can This Marriage Be Saved?' for American Psychological Association, March 7, 2017).

The remedies for marriage outlined in this workbook, *Paradigms of Marriage,* and our seminars provide real strategies to deal with the complex modern companionship marriage.

Chapter One: Love: Pain & Pleasure

Paradigm One: Pit to Paradise
(*Paradigms of Marriage*, pages 1-13)

Happiness denied leads to the **PIT** (Pain, Privation, Problems)
Happiness delivered leads to **PARADISE** (Prosperity, Peace, Pleasure)

"Thou wilt shew me the path of life: in thy presence is fullness of joy; at thy right hand there are **pleasures** forevermore" (Psalm 16: 11).

LONG-TERM PLEASURE/SHORT-TERM PAIN or SHORT-TERM PLEASURE/LONG-TERM PAIN

Most people—Christians and non-Christians—tend to associate spiritual life with pain, denial, sacrifice and non-spiritual life with pleasure, excitement, and ease. Think for a moment about the Bible text above. What is God really offering? PLEASURE! How did the prevailing concept in our society that the worldly life leads to pleasure and the path to Christian perfection leads to pain become entrenched? That is a trick the devil, called Satan, has successfully perpetrated on most of the population of the world. There are many places in the Bible that mention sacrifice as a part of the Christian experience. However, it does so indicating the cost to the sincere seeker is minimal compared to gaining eternal pleasure. The enemy and our sinful nature will cause us to struggle to obtain or maintain God's grace in our lives and live for Him. Here is Paul giving witness to the Biblical perspective:

> Therefore, I take **pleasure** in infirmities, in reproaches, in necessities, in persecutions, in distresses for Christ's sake (2 Corinthians 12:10).

This kind of pain leads to a purposeful end. It ought to be a pleasurable pain. Ask a mother about the pain she suffered in having a baby. The outcome of such a pain brings immense pleasure. Obviously, believing this on a spiritual level requires faith.

Human beings (and, I believe, other living creatures) naturally gravitate toward that which provides pleasure and avoid that which causes pain. Recently, I came upon the program developed by Leo Schreven, a prominent pastor and motivational speaker. He pointed out that when advertising, many industries use the concept of pleasure and pain to sell their products. Regardless of how injurious their products, some businesses promote them as offering pleasure in such a deceptive way that causes the prospective customer's mind to switch from any painful outcome associated with that product and focus only on the temporary pleasure.

IMMEASURABLE CONSEQUENCES

I cannot comprehend how so many people freely use destructive behaviors and products in their quest for pleasure, even though they know the outcome is painful and life threatening. Consider the deadly poison in cigarette that is scientifically proven to cause lung cancer and other physical maladies. Advertisers may use a beautiful woman in an alluring pose with a cigarette between her fingers to deceive customers to purchase and use this dangerous habit-forming product. The image invoked is immense pleasure when you smoke that brand. The reality of a foul poisonous substance that pollutes the lungs, poisons the blood, creates painful health problems, resulting in expensive health costs and sometimes agonizing death is obliterated from the mind. Reality is denied or suspended.

While a business student at Windsor University in Canada, I took a Marketing course. One requirement for the class was to divide up in small groups, discuss an assigned product and develop a viable marketing strategy. The dangers of cigarette smoking were not yet well known to the public. Our group assignment was to develop marketing strategies for a certain brand of cigarettes. Upon researching the known facts at the time, we found that the Sergeant General of the United States had just required that notice of the poisonous effect of cigarette smoking be placed on every pack of cigarette. While discussing this health hazard requirement, we had to develop ideas for selling more cigarettes despite this warning. I looked across at a student in our group who was smoking. Alarmed, I asked him how could he continue to smoke with this clear warning on the package. He just shrugged it off and continued smoking. As a young man, I realized that some people will risk serious long-term pain for the very short-term pleasure.

Not long afterwards that attitude of immediate pleasure became so pronounced in the North American society that a whole generation of youth (during the late sixties and early seventies) was nicknamed the "Now Generation or "Me Generation"." That hedonistic attitude has become pervasive in succeeding generations in North America.

The same goes for premarital sex. Few people, especially among the youth, consider the risks of complicated life-changing problems that often result. We may also consider the devastating effects of social drugs on the body. Despite its visible painful after effects, a large percentage of the North American population has taken social drugs in various forms. Or, consider the possible problems that can ensue when someone cheats on his/her spouse. Yet the lure of present pleasure overrides the prospect of the distress it could cause. From a Christian perspective, that is how Satan deceives us, especially the youth. By subconscious psychological manipulation, the tantalizing sensation of pleasure replaces the rational understanding that pleasure will be short lived and pain and problems will be overwhelming in the future. By this means, the wrong emotion is attached to the action. Leo Schreven recommends that when you make the switch back to reality by attaching the correct emotions to the actions, you will begin to make the right choices. Reason will be allowed to inform emotion.

FREEDOM to CHOOSE

The Bible gives us God's challenge for our lives:

> Behold, I set before you this day a blessing and a curse: A blessing, if you obey the commandments of the Lord your God, which I command you this day: and a curse, if you will not obey the commandments of the Lord your God--- (Deuteronomy 11: 26-28).

APPLICATION for MARRIAGE

The lessons from the foregoing discussion may be easily transferred to marriage because they should be obvious. When we get married, we seek to enjoy a pleasurable experience with our spouse. This may be termed the "Honeymoon" phase. While this experience is being achieved, we feel satisfied. However, when the anticipated pleasurable experience is denied and we feel pain instead, the chances of success become increasingly remote. Our marital goal should be to enhance the happiness of our spouse and seek to secure our own happiness. The purpose of this workbook and *Paradigms of Marriage* is to help couples discover how to avoid the pitfalls that bring pain and follow a path leading to long-term pleasure in their relationship. We offer strategies to grow successful marriages.

Activities

Paradigm 1: Love: Pain & Pleasure

1. 1. List five things in your relationship that cause pain, and five things that give you pleasure.

PAIN

1. _____
2. _____
3. _____
4. _____
5. _____

PLEASURE

1. _____
2. _____
3. _____
4. _____
5. _____

2a Arrange your list of five painful things from least to greatest. Describe how you have attempted to avoid them.

Five things in order from least to greatest: Ways I have attempted to resolve each one:

_____
_____
_____
_____
_____

2b. Discuss with your partner ways that you can both work together to resolve the painful issues that are negative in your life and replace those with more pleasurable ones. Evaluate the outcomes at the end of each two-week period and make adjustments.

3. Assess the following as they affect your relationship, then put an X beside the ones that help you to be happy in the relationship. Discuss these with your spouse or partner:

_____ Romance _____ When my spouse/partner listens without passing judgment _____ When my spouse/partner listens without condemning me _____ A soft answer _____ Intimacy _____ When my spouse/partner works with me to resolve problems _____ When my spouse/partner dialogues with me and is fair and honest _____ When there is a bond of trust between us _____ When my spouse/partner gives me my space and time to reflect _____ Use of loving words and touching _____ Allowing me time to communicate my feelings and sharing his/hers with me

_____ When my spouse/partner is not afraid to take risks _____ When my spouse/partner takes too many risks _____ When my spouse/partner disrespects my family members _____ Bitter quarrels _____ Arguments

4

_____ Arguments that are left unresolved _____ When situations that could have been dissolved keep coming back _____ Physical abuse
_____ Verbal abuse _____ Emotional abuse

4. Plan a rendezvous with your spouse/partner and take turns answering the following true/false questions. Answers are found toward the end of the book.

   a) _____ Romantic love is based on principles.
   b) _____ True love requires time and dedication to develop.
   c) _____ Infatuation can be confused with love.
   d) _____ Unfulfilled expectations do not cause pain and problems in a relationship.
   e) _____ The male partner does not feel the need for security in the relationship.
   f) _____ Couples need God to help them resolve simple problems.
   g) _____ Most families stay together in times of emotional distance, lack of caring, conflicts, financial crises, and stress.
   h) _____ Couples need reassurance from each other that they love each other.
   i) _____ When couples have reached a deep level of intimacy, they may feel secure enough to reveal secrets and personal private information.
   j) _____ When couples share secrets, they lose trust and security in the relationship.
   k) _____ A personal matter, if revealed, may alter the marriage relationship.

5. Please read the following statements and rate the ones which pertain to your relationship with your spouse/partner:

   1. On a scale of 1-10, my relationship with my spouse/partner is _____
   2. If your number is seven or below, list some positive changes you can bring to the relationship to make it better and discuss these together.

   _____
   _____
   _____
   _____
   _____

   If your relationship is above seven, list some ideas of how you can nurture and maintain your relationship for it to reach optimum satisfaction. Discuss the results with your spouse/partner.

   _____
   _____
   _____
   _____
   _____

6. Go to page 7 in *Paradigms of Marriage* and together with your spouse/partner, design your own paradigm for happiness and success in your relationship.

OUR MARRIAGE PARADIGM

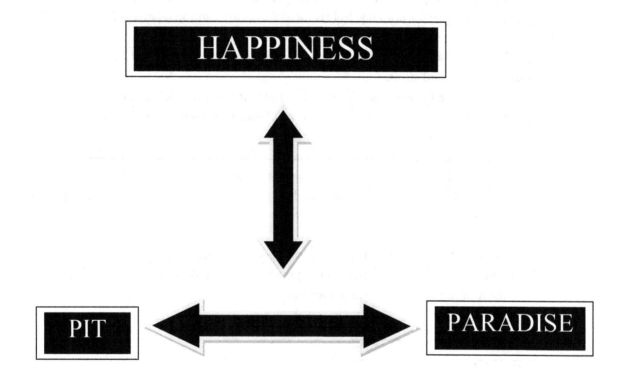

Chapter Two: Commitment

Paradigm Two: Sorting and Satisfying Gender Needs
(*Paradigms of Marriage*, pages 14-29)

Men's needs are very different from the needs of women.
Denial leads to the Pit: Delivery leads to paradise.

> Set me as a seal upon thine heart, as a seal upon thine arm: for love is as strong as death---Many waters cannot quench love, neither can the floods drown it: if a man would give all the substance of his house for love, it would utterly be contemned (Songs of Solomon, 8: 6,7).

MARRIAGE EXPECTATIONS

Most marriages are conducted with the sincere belief that both partners will enjoy a successful relationship for a long period, possibly for life. However, in North America marriages are in crisis. About fifty percent of marriages fail.

Let us ask a key question:

Why do people marry?

Each person may offer a different answer. However, there is one underlying reason most people marry: **HAPPINESS!!** It is based on a natural instinctive motivation for all humans: **we seek to embrace happiness and avoid pain.** Especially in western societies, we conjure up the belief that the highest state of happiness in this life is falling in love with someone who is also deeply in love with us. There is a deep abiding feeling that marrying that person will lead into a state of enduring passionate happiness. This is fantasy intermingled with a good dose of reality. In North America, only about two in ten marriages are likely to have a lasting enjoyable experience. In most other societies, people marry for different basic reasons rather than for love. Usually parents arrange their children's marriage by selecting their spouse. Marriage may be for achieving or maintaining status, preserving family wealth and/or tradition, or preserving culture.

Marrying purely for love presupposes that other fundamental elements for success may be seriously lacking. When the challenges arrive, and they most likely will, the married couple must have a sound commitment to endure and find strategies to reach beyond the difficulties and get back to enjoying the relationship. Better yet, the love between them should remain constant despite the inimical forces they would face.

Since men and women have significantly different needs and most of these needs are often unexpressed or even unknown to the person himself/herself, it would be wise for couples to begin considering the differences between them during the premarital period to discover as much as possible the needs or expectations of the other partner. When we purchase most items, we have an expectation as to how it would be used and how to care for it. Or, we may seek to obtain the information from the accompanying manufacturer's instructions. You should do no less for the one with whom you expect to spend your life or the one with whom you are committed. In fact, this process will lead to a lifelong discovery. Be aware!

MARRIAGE TRANFORMATION

Until the 1970s, marriages were protected by society--civil laws, members of local communities, millennia of marriage traditions, religion, and individuals own expectations—that formed boundaries and aspirations for couples and marriage institution itself. When those boundaries were eroded during the 1960s, marriages were cut adrift. Couples now had few boundaries to protect them from divorce. In the previous traditional system, the laws of the land restricted divorce, allowing only for extreme circumstances but the courts removed those restrictions, allowing couples to divorce for even trivial reasons or none at all. Before the change, marriage statistics could show clearly the reasons for divorce. When the change occurred, most divorces were labelled "irreconcilable differences". In some courts, adultery was not even admitted as a reason for divorce petition.

The society began to accept marital conflicts and divorce as normal. Churches started to ignore divorce issues. Priests, pastors, and parishioners began slowly to accept unfaithfulness in marriage relationships. Hollywood and commercial interests glamorized sex and popularized adultery and promiscuous relationships. Consequently, the communities no longer frowned on those who had marital problems resulting in separation or divorce. Society lowered marital expectations and couples felt free to leave their spouse for reasons they could overcome with little effort. Currently, successful marriages in North America may be as low as ten to twenty percent, with only a percentage of that already small number achieving real fulfillment.

Because of low expectation for the duration of marriages, there is little incentive for couples to commit to each other "until death do us part". Infidelity is rampant and many couples are no longer faithful to the family structure. Ironically, the modern companionship marriage model that promises freedom from the limitations of the traditional model is shackled by limited skills to maneuver successfully through the landmines of problems that await them.

Survival without acquiring skills is extremely unlikely. Under the former system, there were several safeguards to provide support. Now couples are mainly on their own. The tragedy is that most people are not aware that they need skills in negotiation and when they do they are too embarrassed or unwilling to discover how to acquire what they need. Men are notorious for thinking they can handle the relationship without help. Hence, they are most likely to avoid even talking to anyone about their conflicts. Wives often recognize their limitations to resolve the conflicts but cannot persuade their reluctant husbands to seek help. By concealing the conflicts, couples develop an external façade to appear to others that all is well between them. In most cases, it is the proverbial "water under the bridge" when they accept that they will not survive without help. At that point, partners experience painful separation and divorce. Disillusion precedes dissolution.

SKILLS NEEDED

This series is our attempt to alert couples that they need to consider the importance of acquiring skills for healthy marriage growth. Love alone is unable to keep couples together when certain pressures are brought to bear on their relationship. God is able to solve any problem, but because of our human limitations and lack of trust in Divine intervention, even prayers may be ineffective to save some relationships. Marital failure among Church goers closely reflects that occurring in the general population. Even clergy families are not immune from marital break down and failure. **Awareness of skills needed in the modern marriage model is the key.** Couples can then consider learning those skills and growing successful relationships.

PARADIGM 2: GENDER NEEDS

One important skill to be learned is sorting and satisfying gender needs. Men and women are significantly different. Although most people observe some differences, they do not understand what they are and, even more importantly, how to deal with those differences in a daily spousal relationship. Satisfying your spouse's needs is the road to marital "Paradise" but neglecting them will, most likely, lead you into the "Pit" and marital failure.

Special attention should be given to this paradigm. Couples would be wise to sit together and determine the significance of each of his/her needs and share their feelings about them. By discovering the level of need your spouse requires for each, you may adjust your behavior as you relate together. As you satisfy the needs of your spouse, satisfaction in the relationship will most definitely increase. Most marriage partners only guess the level of their spouses need, now they know.

On one occasion, I was counseling a couple with three young children. They could not figure out what went wrong after thirteen years of marriage. They started out in a happy relationship but recently they could not communicate with each other. I gave them the exercise on men's needs and women's needs to fill out privately and bring them to the following session. I cannot forget how the wife reacted when I ask them to exchange sheets for review. When she saw what her husband rated for sexual need for himself and what she rated, she immediately withdrew her rating sheet to make an adjustment, but not before I observed her surprise. The session went very well after we reviewed their responses together and explained how this exercise can help their communication.

Activities

Paradigm 2: Commitment

1. Write your definition of commitment.

   _____

   _____

   _____

   _____

   _____

2. Work separately as you answer the following true/false questions. Compare your answers with your spouse/partner. (See end of book for answers.)

   a) ____ In the marriage relationship, both spouses are expected to fulfill each other's perceived needs.

   b) ____ People who marry expect to be happy.

   c) ____ In some cultures, people marry for different or various reasons other than love.

   d) ____ When I rely on my marriage to fulfill my desire for happiness, I am disappointed if my marriage fails to deliver.

   e) ____ This present age has transitioned into the Romantic marriage-not based on having prescribed roles or functions.

   f) ____ Marriage fulfills all our emotional needs on an on-going basis.

   g) ____ Men and women are different not only physically and regarding predisposition to certain illnesses, but also in terms of personality traits, heredity, and emotional and psychological needs.

   h) ____ According to the author of *Paradigms of Marriage*, marriage can be compared to the design of a house ready to be built rather than a house already built.

   i) ____ Marriage fails when there is not the willingness to face different challenges and there is not an understanding of the nature of the problem.

   j) ____ Because we love each other, we should be able to depend on our spouse to make us happy

3. Why do most couples in North America get married?

   _____

   _____

   _____

   _____

4. Why did you get married?

   _____

   _____

   _____

   _____

5. Are your needs being fulfilled? Why, or why not? Explain.

   _____

   _____

   _____

   _____

6. What plans do you and your spouse/partner have for meeting your unfulfilled needs, if any? Brainstorm, then write your ideas.

_____

_____

_____

_____

7. Has modern America changed its view towards marriage?

_____

8. How do you understand the traditional marriage in terms of roles and leadership?

_____

_____

_____

_____

9. Is your marriage a pattern of the traditional marriage? What stays the same? What is different?_____

10. Read page 20 in _Paradigms of Marriage._ Explain in your own words the three main phases of marriage. Explain each phase separately.

Phase 1: _____

Phase 2:

_____

Phase 3:

_____

11. Using page 24 of the _Paradigms of Marriage,_ list the gender needs in order of importance according to **you**r understanding of the needs of your partner/spouse, then list your own in order of their importance to you. Each should complete the exercise privately. Afterward, compare lists and discuss with each other. Each partner may design a plan for how he/she can improve in meeting his/her partner's needs.

Gender Needs

Needs of My Partner/Spouse My Needs

_____	_____
_____	_____
_____	_____
_____	_____
_____	_____
_____	_____

12. Write 3-5 ways you can <u>prevent</u> your advance to intimacy and 3-5 ways you can <u>increase</u> it.

_____

_____

_____

_____

_____

_____

_____

_____

13. Is marriage a covenant, a contract, or both? Give reasons for your response.

_____

_____

_____

_____

14. Develop a **growth pledge** or use the one provided to design a path for progress in your relationship. Discuss it with your spouse/partner, then sign the pledge, using your spouse/partner as a witness.

_____

'''MY MARRIAGE GROWTH COVENANT
By God's grace,

I pledge to use the principles I have learned from *Paradigms of Marriage* to enhance and grow my relationship with my spouse.

I pledge to use my personal choice option to discover what I can do to enhance the happiness of my spouse and improve our marriage, rather than focusing on my spouse's attitude toward me.

I prayerfully and sincerely petition God's grace to assist me in fulfilling my role as a loving and caring spouse and, thereby, achieving a happy and successful marriage.

Signed:_____Date:_____
      Spouse Making the Covenant

Signed:_____Date:_____
      Spouse/partner as Witness

Signed:_____Date:_____
      Ms. Petula Samms, Marriage Facilitator

Signed:_____Date:_____
      Dr. Robert O. Samms, Marriage Educator

Chapter Three: Conflict

Paradigm three: Ten Paths to the Pit
(*Paradigms of Marriage*, pages 30-41)

Certain behaviors—criticizing, blaming, withdrawing (ignoring), complaining, contemptuousness, threatening, nagging, punishing (denying & abusing), defensiveness, controlling—lead to the **PIT**.

A soft answer turneth away wrath: but grievous words stir up anger (Proverbs 15: 1).
Be you angry, and sin not: let not the sun go down upon your wrath (Ephesians 4: 26).

DISAGREEMENTS

During the period that lovers are experiencing the bliss of early love, they have little concern for the differences between them. Most couples go through that phase. Nevertheless, the differences are there and will emerge sooner or later. When they do, the real challenges begin. At that time, the marriage relationship will be sorely tested. The severity of the test will depend on several factors such as the temperament of the partners, their built-in principles, their spiritual commitment, the depth of their love for each other, their background, their learned coping strategies, their resources such as supporting family members or friends, and the issue/issues involved.

It is important to remember that disagreements between married partners are natural. Everyone is different and enters the relationship with different backgrounds and experiences. Therefore, it is unlikely that two such persons would not have differences. How these differences are handled when they arise is important. Considering that quarrels are inevitable, William Betcher and Robie Macauley said:

> These quarrels are necessary because they are rooted in profound differences the man and the woman understand only dimly. Only by having the quarrel in a new way—without destructive tactics and with a willingness to learn what lies beneath the surface—can it ever be solved (*The Seven Basic Quarrels of Marriage*, pp. 19,20).

Dr. John Gottman found that some marriages even fared better if the partners had early disagreements and avoided destructive tactics.

Some destructive tactics are:
1. When conflicts are accompanied by criticizing, punishing (denying and abusing), controlling, withdrawing (ignoring), contemptuousness, aggression, blaming, nagging, complaining, and defensiveness.
2. When there are frequent hot disputes, accompanied by putdowns and sarcasm.

3. When partners fail to engage each other.
4. When partners start to display lack of trust in each other. (See *Paradigms of Marriage*, p.36.)

After reviewing the literature on destructive behaviors, we have concluded that there are ten basic ones. When couples engage in one or more of these destructive behaviors, they may poison the relationship and bitterness in one or both partners may push them toward the pit. It is important to note these behaviors and avoid them in your relationship.

MAGIC FORMULA

Dr. John Gottman researched and observed couples' responses in a laboratory and concluded that he could predict almost accurately which couples would succeed and which ones would fail based on their behaviors and responses. He arrived at a **formula: 5:1 positive to negative ratio**. If a couple is having five positive experiences to every one negative one between them, the marriage would likely succeed. Here are a few strategies for growing your marriage:

1. Negotiating and accommodating
2. Dialoguing without hostility
3. Short-lived eruptions of passionate disputes
4. Agreeing to disagree
5. Retaining respect
6. Refraining from extreme expression of anger and frustration
7. Investing consistently in your marriage and your spouse, including persistent prayer for each other
8. Avoiding the ten deadly paths to the pit: cherishing the ten paths to paradise.

ADVICE for MEN and WOMEN

Observe carefully the advice of Dr. John Gottman for men and women (*Paradigms of Marriage*, pp. 40,41). Can you see the subtle lesson in the Dagwood and Blondie illustration on page 41? Remember that it is easier to catch a fly with honey than with vinegar.

PARADIGM 3: TEN PATHS TO THE PIT

Give special attention to this paradigm. The ten traits are culled from an array of human behavior. These are critical and fundamental and contribute definitely to the destruction of marriage relationships. Their negative qualities should not be allowed into marriage.

INTIMACY VERSUS CONFLICT

One of the most important goals in marriage is to attain intimacy.

Intimacy is allowing someone to share your inner feelings without fear of being attacked or ridiculed. It is making yourself vulnerable to your spouse.

Think back to the time you first met. Likely, you talked for hours, opening up your inner feelings. You were anxious to share your feelings with your new-found lover.

Many attitudes have changed since the wedding.

WHAT IS CONFLICT? DIFFERENCE BETWEEN RESOLVING AND DISSOLVING

Dr. David Mace defined conflict as difference that becomes an argument, then becomes heated up disagreement.

Dr. Mace mentions four possible responses:

- 1. Avoidance
- 2. Toleration
- 3. Fighting Fair
- 4. Processing (Marriage Enrichment approach).

Better Marriages, Inc. uses the fourth approach as a key strategy in its marriage growth educational program. The process is called **Dialogue.** During Marriage Enrichment sessions, couples are shown by demonstration of the leader couple how to develop and use the dialogue approach. The goal is **dissolving disagreements** and conflicts, not merely **resolving** them.

Resolving a disagreement means the issue is dealt with between the partners to their satisfaction so that the relationship may continue and not be harmed. This may be accomplished by utilizing one or more of the first three approaches above. However, the issue may resurface when a similar situation arises. Dissolving the disagreement requires a process that helps the couple to settle the matter permanently. Knee-to-knee dialoguing using the Marriage Enrichment pattern helps the couple to discover the root cause of the problem and dealing with it in a way that it should not resurface: it would be dissolved, not merely resolved.

Activities

Paradigm Three: Conflict

Most couples may likely experience disagreements that escalate into conflict. It is important to note that arguments may occur because the significant needs of one person may conflict with the significant needs of the other person/partner. Often, the same issues keep recurring.

1. What are some recurring issues that cause disagreements or conflicts in your marriage?

    _____
    _____
    _____
    _____

2. What negative behaviors do you engage in during a quarrel? For example, criticizing, withdrawing, etc.

    _____
    _____
    _____
    _____

List three negative behaviors your partner engages in:

    _____
    _____
    _____
    _____

Important: Spent a few minutes sharing your lists with your partner and dialogue concerning your commitment to avoid them in the future.

3. Check the positive behaviors that apply to you and your spouse.

    Negotiation and compromise   _____
    Negotiation and accommodation   _____
    Dialogue without hostility   _____
    Short-lived eruptions of passionate disputes   _____
    Agreeing to disagree   _____
    Retaining respect   _____
    Refraining from extreme expression of anger and frustration   _____
    Praying consistently for each other   _____

4. Check the negative behaviors that apply to you and your spouse

    Rejecting   _____
    Disapproving   _____
    Disagreeing   _____
    Interruptions   _____
    Defensiveness   _____
    Denial   _____

5. Identify some key personality differences that cause conflict in your marriage.

   _____

   _____

   _____

   _____

6. Identify gender differences that contribute to conflict.

   _____

   _____

   _____

   _____

7. What methods do you currently use to resolve your conflicts?

   _____

   _____

   _____

   _____

8. What strategy will you engage in to increase your chances of dissolving disagreements and conflicts? (refer to page 36 of *Paradigms of Marriage* or the introduction for this section above.)

   _____

   _____

   _____

   _____

Chapter Four: Control

Paradigm Four: Ten Paths to Paradise
(*Paradigms of Marriage*, pages 42-59)

Husband/wife-dominated relationships lead to the PIT.

Egalitarian relationships—negotiating/accommodating, respecting, empowering, cherishing, caring, accepting, encouraging, supporting, listening, loving—lead to PARADISE.

> "Know you not that to whom you yield yourselves servants to obey, his servants you are whom you obey?" (Romans 6:16).
> Submitting yourselves one to another in the fear of God (Ephesians 5: 21).

DEFINITION

The word **control** has several connotations—self-control, controlling another person, controlling something, or being controlled. All of these meanings relate to marriage relationships. One of our most precious gifts as human beings is freedom of choice. Unless incapacitated or in a special helpless situation, no one should surrender his/her freedom to someone else. Although some tradeoffs may be beneficial, the likely outcome is resentment, conflict, and dissatisfaction. When someone exercises power over another person, that power is usually abused over time and the control will not likely be surrendered willingly and, if pressure is applied, power over another person is relinquished only with great drama.

By its nature marriage requires that each partner should surrender some of his/her rights and preferences for the success of the relationship. However, personal responsibility and matters of conscience should not be surrendered. Even the rights and privacy of children should be guarded.

ANGER and AGGRESSION

Men use anger and aggression to humiliate, control, and conquer.

Women are likely to use aggression as a defense mechanism or to retaliate.

Men are more likely to use aggression without anger.

Women use it as a signal of upset.

Men use aggression to instill fear and gain control.

When *women* are upset, they want to talk it through or be left alone.

When **men** are angry, they more likely end the discussion abruptly.

Women may cry to discharge tension and frustration.

Men consider crying senseless because it does little to gain power and control.

Women withdrawing to cry is mainly victimless or does not seek to hurt others.

Men are more likely to avoid intimacy when angry.

Women seek to retain intimacy even when angry.

APPLICATION for MARRIAGE

By understanding these differences, couples could use this information to relate better to each other and prevent escalation of conflict. It may be tempting for partners to use sex to control each other. However, this approach is a double-edged sword. The humiliation and rejection to the aggrieved partner may result in retaliation considering that this is an emotionally charged issue. Marriage requires surrendering to each other to enjoy a shared experience.

The roles of married partners should not include dominance or control. To a large extent, nature has dictated the roles to which each is best suited. Our modern society has various elements that suggest otherwise but even the casual observer should be able to see that men and women are best suited for different roles. Our Creator designed us differently and made plain throughout Scriptures that our happiness and success depend on following His instructions. This is much like a manufacturer's product. The designers and builders know best how the product should be used and cared for in order that the owner may obtain its longest and most enjoyable use. Sometimes the manufacturer may place the instructions in a manual that accompanies the sale of the product. God created us: His manual is the Bible. In it He declares that husband and wife should support each other as a team rather than treat each other as competitors or causing women to function in subservience. As a team, each partner functions in a role for which he/she is best suited (See Genesis chapter 2: 18-24; 3: 16-20; Ephesians chapter 5: 21-33). This egalitarian approach would be more likely to result in a harmonious relationship.

GOD and SEX

Because, to a large extent, God's instructions are no longer heeded in our society, man is looking to his own desires to determine how to live. "There is a way which seems right unto a man, but the end thereof are the ways of death (Proverbs 14: 12).

God gave sex as a gift for husband and wife to join them together in one flesh, but our society has destroyed that divine plan with free sex. Male and female were designed to have children and create families to perpetuate the name and laws of our Creator, but modern society has overthrown God's plan by legally supporting multiple forms of family pattern. Women were entrusted with the gift of bearing children and bringing them up in the fear of the Lord, but now the laws of the land permit women to destroy tens of millions of precious unborn lives. It is estimated that about fifty million unborn babies are aborted around the world every year. By ignoring the sacred use of sex only within marriage, societies have created a problem that is now out of control.

Our purpose is to help as many couples as possible grow healthy, happy, successful families in harmony with God's original plan.

PARADIGM 4: TEN PATHS TO PARADISE

In the previous chapter, we dealt with the ten ways our behaviors may lead to the pit. In this chapter, we view the corollary: ten paths to "Paradise". Happiness will be achieved when couples learn to share control or develop an egalitarian relationship. **Couples should abandon husband or wife dominated relationship and learn to respect, negotiate/accommodate, cherish, empower, care, accept(trust), encourage, support, listen, and love each other.**

TACTICS of SPOUSES

When one partner seeks to dominate the relationship, the weaker spouse may develop coping tactics.

Tactics of the Stronger Spouse

Aggression: controlling, threatening, insulting, ridiculing, becoming violent.

Domination: claiming to be more informed, asserting authority, suppressing spouse's views.

Tactics of the weaker Spouse

External Control: dropping hints, flattering, seducing, reminding the spouse of past favors.

Indirection: pleading, crying, pretending to be ill, acting helpless.

Withdrawing: sulking, generating guilt, playing the martyr, walking away.

TACTICS of EGALITARIAN COUPLES

Negotiation: listening, reasoning, offering trade-offs, surrendering, sharing.

Accommodation: creating room for your spouse's needs when necessary without sacrificing your own: **creating a win/win strategy.**

RELATIONSHIP STRATEGY

A great strategy for dealing with anger: Remember **no one can make you angry**. That is something only you can do regardless of the provocation. Referring to Fred Astaire and Ginger Rogers, Dr. Harriet Lerner said:

> We cannot make another person change his or her steps to an old dance, but if we change our steps, the dance no longer can continue in the same predictable pattern (*The Dance of Anger*, page 14).

When disagreements arise, **STOP**, and consider your part in the conflict. Admit to yourself that you are angry.

- Then, cool down
- Agree not to attack each other when angry,
- Agree ahead of time that when anger occurs, you will work together to process the anger.
- **The key is processing the anger**.
- Use **dialogue** to share your feelings with your partner
- Begin **negotiating** with the view of arriving at an **accommodation,** thereby dissolving the problem.

Consider the Biblical counsel: "Why do you not rather take the wrong? Why do you not rather suffer yourself to be defrauded? (I Corinthian 6: 7). Surrender and seek to accommodate your partner (See Laura Doyle's experience, *Paradigm of Marriage*, pp. 57,58). She wrote:

> As I stopped bossing him around, giving him advice, burying him in a list of chores to do, criticizing his ideas, and taking over every situation as if he couldn't handle it, something magical happened. The union I dreamed of appeared. --- The man who wooed me was back. We were intimate again *(Paradigm of Marriage*, p. 58).

In her book, *The Surrendered Wife*, Laura Doyle helps women to understand that there is more to be gained from a path of reconciliation than one of seeking dominance in the relationship.

Activities

Paradigm 4: Control

Read the Paradigm on Control then answer the questions *(Paradigms of Marriage, p.51)*.

1. In the marriage situation, which of the following would you use to describe control? Put an X beside your answer.
   a) _____ Restricting someone's freedom of choice
   b) _____ Dominating one's partner/spouse
   c) _____ Repressing someone's right to carry out his/her decision/choice
   d) _____ Exercising power over someone's independence
   e) _____ All the above

2. What results are likely to occur from being controlled by one's partner/spouse?

   _____
   _____
   _____
   _____

3. (a) Have you ever felt like your partner/spouse is trying to control you? If so, give an example.

   _____
   _____
   _____
   _____

   (b) How did you react?

   _____
   _____
   _____
   _____

   (c) In what ways did you feel you were being controlled?

   _____
   _____
   _____
   _____

   (d) Do you think that your reactions matched the severity of the problem? Explain.

   _____
   _____
   _____
   _____

   (e) Did you seek resolution(s) to the problem?

   _____
   _____
   _____
   _____

(f) Was the problem dissolved and not come back up again, or did you both find reasonable solutions that allowed your relationship to continue? Describe what happened.

_____

_____

_____

_____

4. Have you ever felt that you have surrendered control regarding decision making to your partner/spouse, or was it a shared experience? Explain.

_____

_____

_____

_____

5. What did it feel like to be controlled or dominated by your partner/spouse? What did you do to loosen the grip and were you successful in doing so? How did you get your freedom back, or didn't you? Describe the situation.

_____

_____

_____

_____

6. (a) Do you believe that marriage partners should each surrender some of his/her own individual rights for the marriage to work? _____

_____

(b) How is this possible? Explain.

_____

_____

_____

_____

7. In the marriage relationship, can the surrendering of one's rights be a positive strategy? When could it be negative? Discuss this with your partner/spouse in an open but non-threatening way. Seek expert help if you are unable to come to a common understanding between you.

_____

_____

_____

_____

8. Imagine that both you and your spouse were trained as leader couples to help other couples learn strategies to maintain a successful marriage. If you were giving them pointers on how not to let themselves be controlled by the other spouse, what would you say to them that you would also say to your partner? Work together and take notes.

_____

_____

_____

_____

9. Respond to this statement: A good/successful marriage requires teamwork.

    _____

    _____

    _____

    _____

10. (a) Have you ever felt that your partner/spouse was actually trying to be your competitor?

    _____

    (b) Why did you feel this way, and what evidence can you provide? For example, your spouse feels he/she is making more money and is trying to exert power in controlling the decision-making in the household.

    _____

    _____

    _____

    _____

    (c) How did you handle the situation?

    _____

    _____

    _____

    _____

    (d) What was the outcome?

    _____

    _____

    _____

    _____

11. Indicate your answer for each statement by writing T for true, and F for false.
    _____ According to *Paradigms of Marriage,* men use aggression to control and dominate women.
    _____ Instrumental aggression and expressive aggression are different.
    _____ Women are likely to use expressive aggression, while men use instrumental aggression.
    _____ In expressive aggression, anger is tinged with fear.
    _____ Instrumental aggression humiliates, controls, and conquer.
    _____ Men are unable to use aggression without being angry.
    _____ Men do not see crying as a strategy women use to gain control.
    _____ Men use aggression to instill fear and gain control.
    _____ Men may engage in passive-aggressive behavior more destructively at home than in the workplace.
    _____ A passive-aggressive male denies a woman her feelings while he focuses on getting his own way.
    _____ Only men are guilty of withholding sex to gain control.

12. Write the ten ways listed in *Paradigms of Marriage* (page 51) that will lead to Paradise.

    _____

    _____

    _____

    _____

13. Can "balancing shared control" in a marriage help lead a couple to marital happiness? How? Discuss this with your partner/spouse and take notes.

   _____

   _____

   _____

   _____

14. What is the concept of "egalitarian marriage" or what does it mean? Go to page 53 in *Paradigms of Marriage* and explain it in your own words.

   _____

   _____

   _____

   _____

15. What are some of the tactics one partner/spouse may use to exert control over the other?

   _____

   _____

   _____

   _____

16. How can couples deal with anger successfully? Read pages 55 and 56 in *Paradigms of Marriage* to answer this question.

   _____

   _____

   _____

   _____

17. Is it better to use accommodation or compromise in a relationship (marriage, or friendship)? Support your answer with details.

   _____

   _____

   _____

   _____

Chapter Five: Accommodation <u>not</u> Compromise

Paradigm Five: Ten Needs of Nature and Nurture
(Paradigms of Marriage, pages 60-74.)

Some traits are hereditary and others are acquired. Identify these traits in yourself and your partner. Prepare to negotiate if differences cause conflict.

And above all things have fervent charity among yourselves: for charity (love) shall cover a multitude of sins (1 Peter 4: 8).

ONE-VOTE SYSTEM

For the traditional marriage, compromise, compatibility, and communication were key factors in resolving or preventing conflicts. Married couples functioned in a system with clear responsibilities and boundaries for husband and wife. Whenever differences arose, the attempt to communicate or compromise would be aided by their respect for the boundaries and responsibilities for husband and wife, father and mother. The husband usually expected and received the courtesy of having the last word. It functioned as a one-vote system.

TWO-VOTE SYSTEM

The functioning of couples in the current system of companionship or partnership relationships rejects the rigid form of that hierarchical pattern. Compromise becomes much more difficult today because both husband and wife cherish and protect their roles as equal partners with equal say in the decision process. In the former system of marriage, the wife would be more likely to surrender through compromise.

Today, the man is more likely to seek for resolution based on accommodation rather than a compromise in which someone surrenders to the other. Skills in negotiation of differences are desperately needed. The real problem for most couples, however, is that they do not possess the necessary skills in negotiation to equip them to handle this difficult art and they are not aware of this indispensable requirement. Young married couples are particularly vulnerable because of their limited exposure to real life experiences. Hence, unresolved conflicts increase significantly resulting in an alarming rise in the number of failed marriages.

ACCOMMODATION NOT COMPROMISE

Compromise is a term commonly used to help couples settle differences. However, the authors believe that compromise does not work best in the current marriage model, although it helped keep couples together under the hierarchical system of marriage when roles were clearly defined. Although compromise seeks to achieve a win/win outcome, that objective may be difficult to achieve because both partners consider themselves leaders. Compromise often requires surrender and sacrifice.

Accommodation is a better strategy for partnership relationships. Couples seek to accommodate each other by making room for the partner's needs without sacrificing one's own.

HUMAN NEEDS

Dr. William Glasser identifies 5 needs of nature (heredity) common to all human beings. They are: **power, freedom, survival, love and belonging,** and **fun**. Both sexes share these five inherited traits. The difference is in the level of need in each trait for each individual. The author of *Paradigms of Marriage* added 5 traits we share from our environment from childhood. Each spouse should seek to ascertain the level of need required for himself/herself, then seek to determine the level of need for your spouse. **Negotiation and accommodation** will be needed in areas of difference to avoid conflict.

ACCOMMODATION

A preferable concept to deal with differences is to seek to ascertain what each other's needs are. Then proceed to negotiate to determine what your partner is comfortable with. Pursue a path of **accommodation**. That means both partners should attempt to accommodate the other person's needs or level of satisfaction. Compromise could lead to the surrender of the weaker party's position in order to gain a peaceful outcome. Or, the one with less to lose in the relationship or less commitment may take advantage of the weaker spouse's position, especially if the stronger spouse is a better negotiator. Therefore, whereas a compromise approach may yield a measure of positive results in the short term, over the long term the partner who surrenders most may begin to experience deep dissatisfaction and unhappiness. **A taker usually keeps taking and a giver usually ends up giving until he/she becomes frustrated because his/her needs are not being met satisfactorily.**

NEED/STRENGTH PROFILE

The need/strength profile offers some clues to understanding the nature of the issues involved between the partners, thereby allowing them another perspective in their search for harmonious resolution to their differences. Take the time to review the **need/strength profile** *(Paradigm of Marriage,* p. 66) and follow the requirements for completing the discovery and comparison of both your ten basic traits. This would lead to a better understanding of yourself and your partner. Those persons considering marriage and those recently married would benefit highly from this exercise. Consider these lines from Laura Doyle:

Vulnerable where she used to be a nag;
Trusting where she used to be controlling;
Respectful where she used to be demeaning;
Grateful where she used to be dissatisfied;
Has faith where she once has doubt *(The Surrendered Wife,* P.20).

Activities

Paradigm 5: Compromise

1. Substitute a word, or phrase for **Compromise.**

    _____
    _____
    _____
    _____

2. Explain your understanding of "compromise" as it relates to the marriage context.

    _____
    _____
    _____
    _____

3. In the marriage relationship, is it better to compromise, or accommodate? Read the information in _Paradigms of Marriage_ on "Compromise" to help you explain the answer (pp. 60-61; pp.69-71; _Workbook_, section above: "Accommodation not Compromise").

    _____
    _____
    _____
    _____

4. What is the meaning of accommodation as it relates to couples in a relationship?

    _____
    _____
    _____
    _____

5. What precedes or comes ahead of the other—compromise, or negotiation?

    _____
    _____
    _____
    _____

6. When could compromise not be a successful path to follow in the context of marriage, or intimate relationships? Read again page 61 in _Paradigms of Marriage_ to provide insight for your answer.

    _____
    _____
    _____
    _____

7. When and how is negotiation a good strategy to use in the relationship with your partner/spouse?

_____

_____

_____

_____

8. What was your belief about compatibility in a relationship with someone planning to get married, or has already been married?

_____

_____

_____

_____

9. After reading pages 63 and 64 in *Paradigms of Marriage,* what do you think now?

_____

_____

_____

_____

10. List the needs of nature and nurture, then dialogue with your spouse in relation to what your needs are. Listen deeply as you take turns talking with each other. Be open about your own feelings then work together in writing a plan that will help you overcome the deficits of which you are now aware. Evaluate your plan as often as needed and make necessary adjustments.

   a) Needs of Nature and Nurture: Arrange the **ten needs** in descending order of importance to you. Do the same for your spouse based on your knowledge or feeling about him/her. Give a **numeric value** (1-5; five being the strongest) to each need for yourself and your spouse. This should be done privately without the knowledge of your spouse/partner. Your partner should do the same. Then compare your results together.

Husband	Wife

c) List the differences you discovered about yourself and your partner:

_____

_____

_____

_____

d) Discuss with your partner a possible plan for overcoming the deficits you discovered (Use negotiation/accommodation as a strategy):

_____

_____

_____

_____

e) Evaluate. Write the adjustments needed (Make sure both of you have an understanding based on accommodation):

_____

_____

_____

_____

11. Write T for true and F for false after reading each statement.
   a) _____ Couples should be aware of each other's level of needs.
   b) _____ Necessary adjustments should be made to benefit the relationship.
   c) _____ People's basic needs may arise from genetic or environmental sources.
   d) _____ Couples in a relationship should acknowledge each other's differences in terms of needs and negotiate/accommodate the differences rather than compromise to meet the needs.
   e) _____ Successful marriage relationship builds a reservoir of emotional support.
   f) _____ Frequently, in a marriage, happiness is achieved by only one person providing nurturing and constant emotional support.
   g) _____ It is necessary for problems in a marriage to be solved right away or as soon as possible.
   h) _____ Since people have different strengths and weaknesses, marriage doesn't have to be 50/50.
   i) _____ Expecting your spouse to take equal share of the responsibilities can create disaster in the marriage relationship.
   j) _____ You should compromise before you negotiate your differences with your partner/spouse.
   k) _____ Using diplomacy in your relationship with your partner/spouse will increase the longevity of your marriage.

12. Read to find the main ideas in *Paradigms of Marriage,* pages 69-74. Discuss these with your partner/spouse, then write a short paragraph to demonstrate your understanding of "negotiation" in the context of your relationship with your partner/spouse.

_____

_____

_____

_____

13. Read the Biblical counsel on pages 72 and 73 in *Paradigms of Marriage.* List some of the main points that apply to your marriage. Discuss them with your partner/spouse.

_____

_____

_____

_____

14. Take a few minutes to relax and reflect on your own life. Dream of something beautiful about yourself (no need to write it, unless you want to).

Chapter Six: Communication

Paradigm Six: Problem to Solution
(*Paradigms of Marriage*, pages 75-90)

Put into action a three-part solution process: determine cause of the problem, analyze the problem, dialogue with partner and apply shared solution.

> For he that will love life, and see goods days, let him refrain his tongue from evil, and his lips that they speak no guile: Let him eschew evil, and do good; let him speak peace, and ensue it (1Peter 3: 10,11).

IS COMMUNICATION GOOD or BAD?

When problems arise in a relationship, communication is usually one of the first areas to be blamed. Most people think that there is not enough communication. However, more communication could mean more problems. Communication is a complex art and, if used incorrectly, could damage relationships. So, Beware!

To be effective, communication between spouses must consider the other person's needs, views, and feelings. It is very important to keep in mind that in the current marriage model communication operates differently from the traditional marriage model. Because couples in the previous system understood their defined roles, they communicated within that system based, to a large extent, on expectations. Today, anything goes. **Any communication between partners in our current system must first pass through the filter of their spouse's feelings at the time**. That opens up much room for misunderstanding and possible conflict. Whereas communication was one of the keys to success for the traditional system, **in our current marriage system, communication may be considered one of the main causes of marriage failure.**

DEFINITION

Communication takes place when a message is sent, received, and understood. This means that both the sender and the receiver of the message should confirm that no distortions occurred during the process and the transmission took place as intended. Much care should be taken to develop the art of effective communication.

EMOTIONAL CURVES

Men and women have distinctly different emotional curves. Because of their difference in sexual orientation, men and women experience life differently, not only in their sexual experiences, but also in their everyday existence. These differences in their emotional cycles provide the basis for unexpected misunderstanding and even conflict. Both partners would benefit from an understanding of how these emotional cycles operate in men and women and be prepared to deal with the effect of these differences by making allowances for their spouse's moods and responses. (See *Paradigms of Marriage*, p.79ff.)

GENERALIZED DIAGRAM: EMOTIONAL CURVES

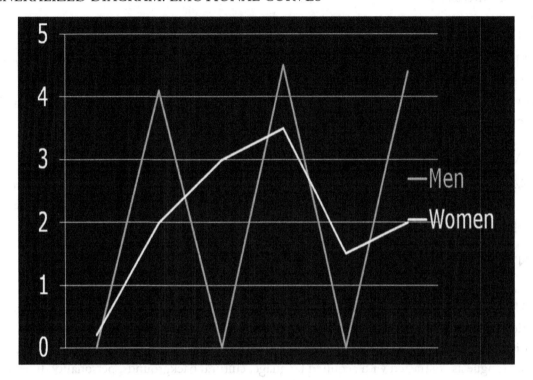

CRITICAL DIFFERENCES

Based on the significant differences between the sexes, emotional fluctuations as seen in the diagram above could lead to frequent conflicts because of the differences in the levels of the couple's emotions. One spouse may be at the peak of his/her emotions while the other is at the bottom. They may not be aware that their problem at the time may be rooted in their biology, their emotional difference. **Husbands must bear in mind that women are particularly prone to emotional fluctuations, especially during certain times and events in their lives.** Great effort must be made by both spouses to take into consideration each other's needs and feelings, **especially as they enter different decades in their growth, bodily changes, and pressures of life**.

It is easy for the wife to feel her husband is not sensitive to her feelings and for the husband to think he is being ignored. That is when the temptation to consider the grass on the other side of the fence as being much greener than yours. **Patience and understanding with each other will prove to be more valuable when you realize you have conquered another mountain together, rather than yield to the temptation of a fleeting fling of passion with someone else.**

Do not assume your spouse knows what you are going through. Even if he/she knows, you cannot experience the other persons deep feelings. They are unique to that person. You can only try to understand and make room for what you cannot fully experience. **Remember to verbalize your feelings to your spouse**, unless you are sure he/she can read your mind. **Practice Dialogue!**

When problems arise, one way to deal with them **is to cool off, discover the cause of the problem, analyze it, and dialogue** with your spouse to reach a shared solution. Then, apply it. This approach could lead to a closer relationship and growth in emotional bonding. **Be aware of your emotional differences from time to time and be prepared to deal with them or make allowance for these differences**.

LANGUAGE

Men and women use language differently. Sometimes women talk to sort out their feelings in order to feel better. Men talk with the goal of solving a problem. That's the reason they try to solve their wife's problems when their wives only want them to listen. **<u>Listening deeply means listening without passing judgment, offering advice, or attempting to fix a problem</u>**.

PARADIGM 6: THREE-PART SOLUTION

When problems arise, discover the cause or source of the problem, then analyze it, and proceed to develop a solution. A strategy to help arrive at a solution: **organize, prioritize, and share** with your spouse. Both should **dialogue** to help develop a solution.

MEN'S MISTAKE and WOMEN'S TASK

Valuable counsels are given on pages 86-88 in *Paradigms of Marriage*. Review them.

Always bear in mind that communication can be distorted because of many reasons: childhood experiences, forming character patterns that influence behavior, use of language, especially semantical variations, facial expressions, the setting, mood of the partners, thereby influencing the tone, one's mother tongue as contrasted with acquired language, cultural backgrounds, personality differences, and so on.

Because men use language to effect outcomes and women use language frequently to sort out their feelings and seek intimacy, men often complicate the issue when they try to analyze, ignore, or comment negatively on their wife's experiences or concerns. They may also try to solve their wife's concerns without being asked.

PERSONAL STORY

Robert, the author of *Paradigms of Marriage*, was constantly challenged regarding offering to solve Petula's concerns. When Petula begins to talk about a concern, I would immediately go into the mode of offering to solve it. I may even reflexively down play the issue so that Petula would minimize it. But she doesn't! In fact, that approach would make it worse because she thinks that I am not listening to her and/or doesn't really care about that concern. Now I have the problem of trying to fix the new problem I created.

Men need to listen deeply without interrupting, thereby allowing their spouse to feel she has expressed her feelings. If she requests it, dialoguing with her may help her find a solution. Greater intimacy will develop in that atmosphere of trust and understanding. After my four years of marriage to Petula, I am still working on that and other issues.

On the other hand, women are impatient with men and tend unknowingly to push them into a difficult corner. Men don't want to lose and they become very defensive easily. Maybe they are just trying to protect their manhood. Then, too, by nature men tend to escalate to anger when under stress. Wives should use their feminine graces to soothe him or wait until he cools off before approaching him with an issue, concerns about his faults, or even some duty she wants him to perform. That's when some men lose control and could even be physical. Ladies, when your husband is angry or frustrated, especially if it is about you, if you don't choose to soothe him, leave him alone. **Give him time to cool down.** At the appropriate time, try to engage him in the Marriage Enrichment strategy of "dialogue".

Wives may also need to remember that when she is expressing her concern to her husband, especially if it is about him, she would be wise to give him a chance for occasional response. If she launches into a lengthy "tirade", he may become impatient and tune out or get angry, especially if he thinks the concern is unfair to him. Unless the matter is urgent, try to wait until the angry partner cools down and the time is right to approach your spouse/partner.

Activities

Paradigm six: Communication

Communication is one of the keys to a successful marriage. To be effective, communication between spouses must take into account that our partner does not know exactly what we are thinking and feeling. We must explicitly express what we want our partner to know.

1. Rate your satisfaction level of communication with your spouse on a scale (10 being the highest and 1 being lowest).

   _____

2. Describe your present communication with your partner. Use a check to select the phrase that applies.
   a) Communication with my partner is frequent and effective. _____
   b) Stress negatively impacts our communication. _____
   c) Deep listening is a skill my spouse has mastered. _____
   d) My spouse moodiness directly impacts our communication. _____
   e) Financial difficulties impede our communication. _____
   f) I can communicate without fear of criticism/ judgment from my spouse. _____
   g) Anger prevents me from communicating in a careful nurturing manner. _____

3. List those things that increase your ability to communicate effectively with your spouse.

   _____
   _____
   _____
   _____

4. List those things that present barriers to communication with your spouse.

   _____
   _____
   _____
   _____

5. Explore some gender differences that may prevent your flow of communication.

   _____
   _____
   _____
   _____

6. There are some techniques that can improve/increase communication. Rate your ability to communicate based on the following things:

	Always	*Sometimes*	*Never*
a) Offering self (take time to communicate feelings and thoughts)	_____	_____	_____
b) Patience (when partner is communicating)	_____	_____	_____
c) Understanding (compassion and thoughtfulness)	_____	_____	_____
d) Deep listening (listening with your heart)	_____	_____	_____
e) Accepting (giving indication that there is no judgment about what is being said)	_____	_____	_____

36

f) Restating (repeat the main idea expressed)   _____ _____ _____

g) Encouraging (spouse to communicate fully)   _____ _____ _____

h) Exploring (exploring further what is being said)   _____ _____ _____

i) Focusing (on main point of concern or interest)   _____ _____ _____

j) Reflecting (re-stating what is being said)   _____ _____ _____

k) Validating (conveying a deep understanding and acknowledgement of what is being said)

_____ _____ _____

7. Describe a successful day with your spouse/partner. What activities make up that day. You can start the description with the sentence *I feel best when…*

_____

_____

_____

_____

8. What do you expect from your spouse/partner when you communicate? Be very specific.

_____

_____

_____

_____

Be sure to share your expectations with your spouse/partner.

9. We must be careful not to assume what our spouse/partner is saying or judge his/her reaction without attempting to clarify. See below a few examples of phrases that may have built-in assumptions. "You never listen to me". This sentiment may really mean that "I am not feeling heard" as opposed to not taking the time to listen.
    "I can't read your mind". May really indicate that what is being said is not very clear.
    Explore some assumptions you may have about your spouse/partner. Re-phrase.

_____

_____

_____

_____

10. You can make a conscious effort to use your deeper knowledge of your spouse/partner to increase communication with him/her. Describe some new strategies you can employ to strengthen communication with your him/her.

_____

_____

_____

_____

11. Active listening is a key component of communication. Speak to your spouse about a matter that is important to you. Now invite your partner to repeat what you said. Was it what you intended to communicate? Rate your spouse on how well he/she **heard** you.

Now it's your spouse's turn.

Chapter Seven: Children

Paradigm Seven: From Willing to Acting
(*Paradigms of Marriage*, pages 91-107)

Reveal the process of decision-making.

> For you shall eat the labor of your hand: happy shall you be, and it shall be well with you. Your wife shall be as a fruitful vine by the sides of your house: your children like olive plants round about your table (Psalm 128: 2,3).

PARENTAL DUTY

Most families consider a happy life to be father, mother, and children interacting loving and harmoniously in a peaceful, pleasant, and comfortable home. Yet the reality is that few families attain even a reasonable measure of such a setting. There are conflicts between husband and wife, parents and children. This distressful situation continues until something breaks, perhaps the marriage ends in divorce or the children leave home prematurely and unprepared for a successful life.

Much of the stresses and conflicts occur because parents lack the necessary skills to maintain and grow their relationship and lack the skills to protect and guide their children. Nancy Van Pelt made these remarks:

> Three feelings a child senses significantly affect his comprehension of self-worth: **uniqueness, belonging, and human love**. These three feelings combine to give stability and support to the structure of the self-concept. If one of these three aspects [is] weak, to the same degree the developing self-concept will also be weakened (*Train Up a Child*, pp. 32,33).

YOU HAVE WHAT IT TAKES

John Eldridge shares valuable insights regarding a father's responsibilities toward his children. In his book, *You Have What It Takes*, he pointed out that every father is duty bound to answer positively over and over his son's life-changing question: "Do I have what it takes"? In the same manner, every father must answer repeatedly his daughter's passionate question: "Am I lovely"? Eldridge insisted that the future of a father's children is shaped largely by how he responds to his children's yearning for his approval and reinforcement (*Paradigms of Marriage*, p. 91). A child's mother has a different role. Her nurturing, loving, and responding to the child's needs are unrivaled. Remember the saying: "The hand that rocks the cradle rules the world"? It is still very true!

LESSON IN PARADIGM 7

Special attention must be given to the lesson in paradigm seven *(Paradigms of Marriage,* p. 95). The mental process that occurs subconsciously or consciously takes place whenever we perform an action. Habits formed over time contribute to a pattern of behavior causing us to act spontaneously with little or no conscious thought.

Consider this illustration: Robert and Pamela had moved from their home in Jacksonville to a temporary apartment until they could move into a new home. A few days after they moved, Robert explained that he had driven her to the grocery store and they were returning home. They were talking pleasantly together when suddenly he realized that he had driven to the house from which they had recently moved without any conscious thought. His subconscious activity in his brain led him to the former residence, not their new home. They laughed about the incident but it illustrates that most of our actions each day are reflexive rather than conscious decisions and actions.

Scientists have concluded that about ninety percent (90%) of our actions are influenced by our subconscious process, only about five to ten percent (5-10%) may be influenced directly by our conscious decisions. **That means even the actions we perform consciously may be preconditioned by our habits that previously formed patterns in our brain. Scary thought!**

ACTIONS BY REFLEX

We have built patterns in our brain that cause us to respond in a reflexive manner without thought process when prompted by repeated stimuli. Neurological scientists at Johns Hopkins University have been able to track voluntary activity in the brain (See Johns Hopkins research findings: *"What Free Will Looks Like in the Brain"* (released July 13, 2016). Using Functional magnetic resonance imaging (fMRI) technique, they observed the brain patterns while the subject makes voluntary and involuntary decisions. The report states:

> For the first time, researchers were able to see both what happens in a human brain the moment a free choice is made, and what happens during the lead-up to that decision — how the brain behaves during the deliberation to act.

RESEARCH FINDINGS CONFIRM THE BIBLE

Researchers at Johns Hopkins also found that when a response to a particular stimulus is repeated a few times, a discernable path is made in the brain that prompts the same response or behavior subconsciously. That's the reason people can lie without recognizing they are lying. The behavior is built in the brain by a neurologically visible path. After building a pattern, we may lie or perform other activities by pure reflex. The same applies to good/bad decisions and moral/immoral behaviors. We respond by what our habits dictate. Frightening! The Bible is ahead of revealed science once again. If we dwell on certain thoughts or rationally commit to certain behaviors, a positive pattern is formed in certain areas of the brain that control decisions and actions. This helps us respond positively when certain decision-making situations emerge. The Bible counsels:

> ---whatsoever things are true, whatsoever things are honest, whatsoever things are just, whatsoever things are pure, whatsoever things are lovely, whatsoever things are of good report; ---think on these things (Philippians, chapter 4: 8).

James Dobson said that a relationship that is characterized by genuine love and affection is likely to be a healthy one, even though some parental mistakes and errors are inevitable (*Marriage and Family*, p.82). Romans chapter 12: 1-2 (quoted below) conveys the salient point that our immoral minds can be reprogrammed to do right habitually.

The process of making decisions and subsequently acting is often based on subconscious patterns formed in the brain. When we expose ourselves to certain influences and images, we build patterns in our brain that reflect in our behaviors. (See R. Samms, *Paradigms of Marriage,* pages 95-96 for more details). We can now see clearly the reason watching bad conduct on the television, such as senseless murders, indiscriminate violence, illicit sex, and social drugs, including smoking, will have a deleterious effect on young and old alike. We tend to act out what is embedded in the subconscious. For Christians, that explains why God gives us a law, His word, prayer, and worship to help us form good patterns in our subconscious. **Consider this Biblical appeal:**

> I beseech you therefore, brethren, by the mercies of God, that you present your bodies a living sacrifice, holy, and acceptable unto God, which your reasonable service. And be not conformed to this world: **but be transformed by the renewing of your mind**, that you may prove what is that good, and acceptable, and perfect will of God (Romans, chapter 12: 1-2).

STRICT PARENTAL GUIDANCE

Parents must help these impressionable minds to build correct behavior patterns in the minds of their children so that even their subconscious reactions to their impulses will be controlled and their actions will be positive. Music, television, video and computer games, with their excessive sexual images and violence are main sources of forming patterns in children's impressionable minds. That is the reason, they need strict parental guidance at all times. Otherwise, they will reflexively act out the negative impressions formed in their minds, consciously or subconsciously.

Parents should provide sources of help for their children to develop educated reason and sensitive conscience. If the reason and conscience are poorly developed or silenced, children may grow up to be immorally uncontrolled adults, perpetrating heinous crimes on their society—human beings, animals, and the environment. To the contrary, those children whose reason is positively trained and conscience wholesomely sensitized will grow into morally responsible adults. The Bible provides guidance for both reason (through His Law) and conscience (through the Holy Spirit).

DIAGRAM: HOW ACTIONS ARE FORMED

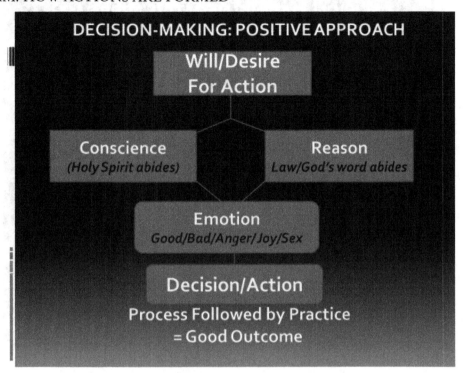

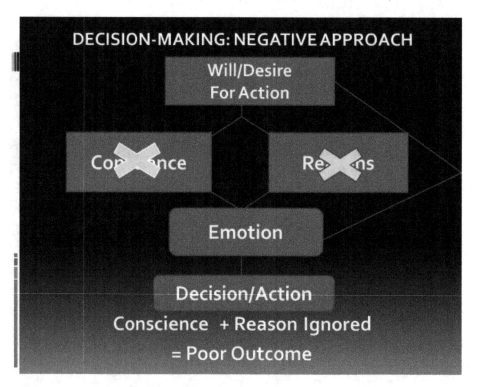

BIBLE TEXTS

Will: John 1: 12,13; Revelation 22: 17
Conscience: 1 Timothy 4:2; Romans 9:1;
        Ephesians 4:30.
Reason: Isaiah 1: 18,19
Emotions: Ephesians 4: 26,27
Decision: I Peter 1: 23; Isaiah 30: 21.
        Deut. 11: 26-28.

Most of our actions are influenced by the subconscious portion of the brain, through habits we have already formed.

CAUTION

Parents should teach their children not to act purely on their emotions. Children should practice educating their decisions by passing them consciously through their reason and conscience until they develop wholesome habits. If parents want their children to grow up as Christians, they must expose them to wholesome Christian education when they are forming their habits, that is, up to twelve years old.

When children, and even adults, are constantly exposed to violence, explicit sexual activities, deceitful conduct, cheating, intemperance, social drugs, smoking, alcohol, unhealthy environment, pornography, immoral behavior, inordinate quest for fame and wealth, marital unfaithfulness, and sexual promiscuity, their brain will begin to form patterns of acceptance and normalcy for those behaviors. This results in a behavior conditioning that leads the person to accept those behaviors as normal. When sufficiently exposed to those lifestyles, even a person who was taught to be honest and moral would defend and, likely, yield to those practices.

ILLUSTRATION: SUBLE CONFORMITY

While their children were in their early teens, Robert and Pamela invited one of their nephews to live with them. He was thirteen, the same age as their oldest child. He arrived from Jamaica with a collection of music, including Reggae that was breaking into the North American music world. Not only did the children not like it they resented when it was played in the house. About two weeks later, we noticed that they not only accepted Reggae but they were enjoying it. Most if not all of us are subject to conditioning.

LESSON LEARNED:

Expose ourselves and our children to that which is noble and uplifting and avoid looking at or participating in anything that is immoral and corrupting. One writer has said: "Shun the appearance of evil". Another true saying: "By beholding we become changed." And the counsel of Solomon: "Keep thy heart with all diligence; for out of it are the issues of life."

Activities

Paradigm 7: Children

Here are a few questions to get started:

 ➢ Do you have children? _____
 ➢ How old is the oldest? _____
 ➢ The youngest is what age? _____
 ➢ Are the rules in your home the same for each child? Why/why not?

_____

_____

_____

_____Do you use corporal discipline?_____

 ➢ When do you not use corporal discipline?

_____

_____

_____

_____

 ➢ Do you love all your children equally? Explain:

_____

_____

_____

_____

 ➢ When, as parents, you have differences of opinion in how children should be disciplined for any particular act, how do you handle the situation? Do you compromise, communicate, negotiate, keep silent? What?

_____

_____

_____

_____

 ➢ What ideals do you have for your children?

_____

_____

_____

_____

After reading the paradigm on children, write what is fact and what is opinion-F for fact and O for opinion.

 a) _____ A father can shape his child's future by how he responds to his/her yearning for approval and reinforcement.
 b) _____ A mother has strong influence on her child's formative years of development.
 c) _____ You should not deny your children the freedom to respectfully disagree with your views on issues.

d) _____ Every child is different.

e) _____ An impoverished childhood can lead to loneliness, self-hate, and personal misery.

f) A child needs to experience human love and feel a sense of belonging.

g) _____ Corporal discipline should end when a child reaches age 10.

h) _____ It is all right to have disagreements in the presence of your child/children.

1. Select any two of the statements below. Write your disagreement(s) and agreement(s) on the views, or issues in separate columns, then, as a couple, discuss how you will accommodate each other's views/or come to a common understanding, if different.

    a) Children need to exemplify their own values, not their parents'.

    _____
    _____
    _____
    _____

    b) Children don't need corporal discipline to correct their inappropriate behavior(s).

    _____
    _____
    _____
    _____

    c) When children are unwilling to reason, parents should apply corporal discipline.

    _____
    _____
    _____
    _____

    d) Read pages 95-101 in *Paradigms of Marriage*, then answer the question: Can children be trained to use their reason and conscience to make right decisions and act accordingly? Explain.

    _____
    _____
    _____
    _____

    e) What happens when an individual performs an action without passing it through the reason and the conscience?

    _____
    _____
    _____
    _____

2. What is the moral basis for decision making? Read from page 100 in *Paradigms of Marriage*, then write a short paragraph.

    _____
    _____
    _____
    _____

3. Describe your parental responsibilities, then discuss these with your children/or spouse. Be willing to listen and make the changes necessary for improving the relationship. Plan weekly meetings (or as needed) to evaluate the outcome(s) and receive feedback.

My Parental Responsibilities: _____
_____
_____
_____
_____

Changes Necessary: _____
_____
_____
_____
_____

Expected Outcome(s): _____
_____
_____
_____
_____

Feedback:
_____
_____
_____
_____

4. These are questions for assessing the job you do as parents: Take turns discussing the points you make. Listen without one condemning the other. Support and strengthen each other as you continue the job.

a) Do you consider yourself a good parent?
_____

b) What are you lacking in your behavior(s) as a parent?
_____
_____
_____
_____

c) If you consider yourself lacking in parenting skills, will you seek help?
_____

d) What mistakes have you made in your parenting job? Pick a few and list them.
_____
_____
_____
_____

e) Have the mistakes you made affected your child/children? How?

_____

_____

_____

_____

f) Did you, as a couple, discuss the mistakes? What conclusions did you arrive at?

_____

_____

_____

_____

g) Do the children know about the mistakes? Under what circumstances did you tell them and how did they respond? Explain.

_____

_____

_____

_____

h) Do you and your spouse/partner share the same values? What is different and how do you handle differences?

_____

_____

_____

_____

i) Do you show your children respect and how do you model this behavior?

_____

_____

_____

_____

Chapter Eight: Family Finance

Paradigm 8:
The Debt Trap versus Financial Freedom
(*Paradigms of Marriage,* pages 108-123)

Debt is the path to the PIT: debt free is the path to PARADISE.

"Owe no man anything, but to love one another" (Romans, chapter 13:8).
"He that loves silver shall not be satisfied with silver; nor he that loves abundance with increase" (Ecclesiastes, chapter 5: 10).
A man's life consists not in the abundance of things which he possesses (Luke 12: 15).

MONEY and MARRIAGE

An estimated one-third of the sayings of Jesus recorded in the Gospels refer to money or wealth. If Jesus spent so much time talking about money, we should seriously consider its effect on our lives. In today's society, we are pressured on every side to consider money as central to our lives. Even several prominent church leaders influence their hearers with the enchanting concept of wealth as a legitimate goal for Christians. No wonder then that many couples find money matters a common area of constant conflict. In fact, apart from infidelity and tragedy, I can't think of anything more challenging to married couples and families than finances. Whether there is a lot of money available or a lack of it, serious issues may arise.

The purpose of this topic is to focus on the concept of getting out and staying out of debt. This problem is critical for so many homes. Those who have sufficient funds for their family needs may have other types of financial issues. They may have to deal with how their family brought them up with regards to getting and spending money. One spouse may have a commitment to spending frugally even if more than adequate funds are available and the other spouse may be brought up with the concept of purchasing to satisfy certain perceived needs whether funds are limited or in surplus. The couple must learn to adjust to each other's disposition or temperament in order to avoid friction and conflict.

MONEY AND MARITAL PROBLEMS

Because women have entered the workforce in large numbers and sought salary parity with men, equal work for equal pay, some may even obtain higher income than their husbands. This may create a new problem in the relationship. Not only will there be a temptation for the woman to use her long desired financial freedom to act independent of her husband, she may use it to seek to dominate her partner in matters of decision making. Feeling humiliated, he may seek to retaliate, thereby increasing tensions in the relationship. This issue was much less important in the traditional period of marriage. Financial disagreements have now risen to the top issue among the causes of marital conflicts. Anna Miller wrote:

> **Another factor is finances.** A 2009 report from the University of Virginia's National Marriage Project, for example, showed that couples with no assets are 70 percent more likely to divorce within three years than couples with $10,000 in assets. That comes as no surprise to Terri Orbuch, PhD, of the University of Michigan and Oakland University, who says arguments over money — how to spend, save and split it — plague even well-off couples. In her work with the Early Years of Marriage Project, a longitudinal study of 373 couples who married in 1986 (funded by the National Institutes of Health), Orbuch has found that seven out of 10 pairs name finances a cause of relationship trouble. "Money is the No. 1 source of conflict or tension," she says (Anna Miller, "Can This Marriage be saved?" written for American Psychological Association, posted by Lauren McRae, March 7, 2017).

WHAT IS DEBT?

Some people consider that they are in debt only when their salary cannot meet their expenses. However, when that occurs, their financial situation may have already reached a critical stage. For instance, if someone has many debts accumulated by credit cards and various consumer loans and he/she could pay the monthly payments comfortably, he/she may think all is well. However, when a change in income or some unexpected expense occurs, disaster could be impending. At that point, what now becomes evident was already like a volcano waiting to erupt. Those who are rich are not exempt because it is possible for anyone to experience unexpected reversal of fortune. Many people get into debt without thinking seriously about it until the debt becomes an issue. **Debt should be shunned like a plague.**

> **Debt is any amount of cash you borrow without putting up collateral;**
> **Any credit extended to you;**
> **Any service you take without paying for it at the moment you receive it.**

PREPARING for RETIREMENT

Perhaps the most devastating effect of living in debt occurs when someone can no longer earn. This could occur for various reasons, expected and unexpected. We all know that if we live long enough, we get old and the body cannot take the strain and stress of regular work. Unexpected illness may happen to anyone at any time, removing him/her from the workforce. If sufficient preparation was not made during working years, life could become extremely stressful and poverty may ensue. Couples need to provide for their later years and not depend on their children or other family members to come to their aid because those resources may not be available when the need is greatest.

STRATEGIES to LIVE DEBT-FREE

Simple practical exercises are presented to assist anyone to evaluate his/her finances and develop ways to embark on a path of getting out of debt and living debt-free.

The Activities in this section will assist even those not inclined to dealing with financial figures to follow and obtain needed assistance. The objective is to learn and practice a sound financial strategy. This chapter will help you evaluate your spending habits, ascertain your financial condition by looking at your assets and liabilities to determine your true net worth, and recommend a healthy path forward.

REMEMBER

Remember, you cannot force your spouse or anyone else to live debt-free. You are responsible only for your own actions. Once you understand how to live debt-free, you may then share the principles with your spouse and seek his/her support. Action is indispensable if you want to achieve financial freedom.

PERSONAL ADVICE

Here are a few tips to help you along the way with your finances. If you choose to maintain a credit card for convenience and to maintain a good credit, try to keep only one card and keep the balance low or pay it off monthly. Consider the following advice from a contributor to Credit.com:

> Maintaining a personal checking and savings account gives you peace of mind. You spent some time on your own and got used to managing your own money, and maintaining a personal bank account provides you with some control. Keep a separate credit card account of your own for maintaining and building solid credit. Holding your own bank accounts allows you to feel secure and allows you to manage some of your money how you prefer.

> Talk regularly with your spouse and make tweaks as needed with your finances. Regular communication and having a plan makes your money work for your marriage rather than causing arguments. Agreeing on how to manage your new family's finances in advance of marriage allows you to start out your new marriage on a solid foundation (Beth Kotz, "Unique Financial Challenges That Arise in a 2nd Marriage", posted by Lauren McRae, February 27, 2017).

SAVING FOR THE FUTURE

Most people know the importance of saving for the future, especially for the retirements years. Unfortunately, most youth do not think that far ahead. As a result, they do not start to save in earnest until later in life. Because there is no sense of urgency about saving, the money that is saved casually may be squandered or spent easily when needs arise. That occurs during the times of hardship such as when someone is out of employment for a while or returns to college to obtain additional education.

However, if young people only knew how easy it would be to accumulate significant savings by starting early and being consistent with even a small amount of saving, they would commit themselves to it enthusiastically. For example, investing $100.00 per month beginning at age twenty would yield about $186, 250 by retirement age. This is based on the average stock market investment yield over past years. Parents need to encourage their children to start saving early.

Activities

Paradigm 8: Family Finance

Please read Chapter 8 in *Paradigms of Marriage* before answering the following questions.

1. Does money play a major role in how you function as a family? Cite some specific reasons for your answer.

   _____

   _____

   _____

   _____

2. How do you teach your teenagers, or younger children to handle money?

   _____

   _____

   _____

   _____

3. If you are a user of credit cards, how do you handle payments without stress and hardship on your finances?

   _____

   _____

   _____

   _____

4. Are there months when your expenses are more than your income? How do you account for that? Describe the situation.

   _____

   _____

   _____

   _____

5. Study the Paradigm on page 111. Do you find yourself getting into debt? How can you best deal with your debts? Write your ideas separately from your spouse/partner, then discuss your findings together.

   _____

   _____

   _____

6. **Planning A Debt Free Future:** The following exercises are based on instructions given on pages 112-120 in *Paradigms of Marriage*. Please follow the guidelines below carefully. Define the following terms:

   ➢ Debt

   _____

   _____

➤ Liabilities

_____

_____

➤ Assets

_____

_____

A. **Decide firmly that you want to live debt free**. Discuss this idea with your spouse/partner. Then decide to stop spending, except for recurring bill payments, large purchases (house and auto), and living expenses.

B. **Cut up all credit cards immediately.** (Do not include debit cards or bank cards.) If you feel insecure, then keep one card but place it in a place where you will not have easy access to it. One suggestion is to place it in a plastic container with water and put it in your freezer. You may also consider a prepaid credit card.

C. **Make a list of <u>all the money that your family spent</u>** for the previous month. (You want to ascertain precisely where the money goes each month.) Include everything you spent money for, such as regular recurring bills, a sandwich for lunch, bus tickets, monthly bus pass, donation, gas, credit cards, etc. Add up the amounts. Deduct the total from your income. Which is larger?

Income (one month)	Expenses (one month)
Totals = Income $	**Expenses $**
Difference:	

D. Make an Assets and Liabilities statement. (This will determine your exact financial situation.) Let's begin. Assets are what you **own**: Liabilities are what you **owe**. (See *Paradigms of Marriage*, pages 118, 119.)

Assets	Liabilities
Totals = $	$
Difference $	$

Deduct the smaller from the larger. If the assets column is larger, your **net worth** is the difference. This means you are financially solvent and able to pay your recurring expenses. If the liabilities column is larger, you are insolvent. This means that should you die in that financial condition and all you own are sold, your funds would not cover all your debts. In other words, you would be bankrupt. Let's take action and change the situation into a positive financial status.

E. Make a list of all your monthly Payments. (Do not include regular expenses only those you owe to a creditor, such as credit cards, mortgage, car payment.) Now you are ready for the **Snowball Approach.** Use the list of your expenses you made up previously. List all payments from smallest to largest after determining the minimum payment you are permitted to make on each one.

EMERGENCY FUND

Before you begin paying off your debts, you should set up an emergency fund. Determine the amount you may need depending on your situation. We suggest between $1000.00 to $2000.00. If you don't have the cash on hand begin to save for it. If your situation is desperate, see if you can find something in your home to sell. Remember you are on a mission to become debt-free. Temporary sacrifice may be required to accomplish your goal.

SNOWBALL PAYMENT PLAN
(List all bills from smallest to largest)

Debts	Amount Owing	Smallest Payment

F. **Begin payment plan by paying off the smallest first**. Then add that payment amount to the next smallest bill. Repeat the same for the next smallest after the previous one is paid off. Larger and larger amounts will be paid on the next smallest bill until they are all paid. (See *Paradigms of Marriage*, p.120.) Remember to make the minimum payment on all the bills, except the smallest. Use all available funds, including the amount you were paying on the previous smallest bill, to pay on the smallest. If you follow this plan faithfully, you and your family will soon be out of debt. It does not matter how long it takes, providing you are following the plan. Each month you will be one month closer to becoming debt-free. Then you can spend cash for what you need and develop an investment plan for the future.

7. Read scenarios one and three on pages 122 and 123, then write your own scenario.

_____
_____
_____
_____
_____
_____

8. **Work together with your spouse/partner and develop a spending plan**. You may invite your child/children to participate. Use an extra sheet of paper, if necessary.

MONTHLY SPENDING PLAN

Bills to be paid	Payment Amount
	Total = $

Monthly Income = $ _____

Savings = $ _____

9. Write a family financial contract and include input from your immediate family members (spouse/partner/children). If you have under age children, include them, too. Not only will they learn, they will cooperate more easily with the objective.

Our Family Financial Contract

_____

_____

_____

_____

_____

_____

_____

_____

_____

_____

_____

_____

Signed:

Father _____ Date: _____

Mother _____ Date: _____

Chapter Nine: Sex & Intimacy

Paradigm Nine: Law of Diminishing Returns
(*Paradigms of Marriage*, pages 124-147)

Know the difference between sex and intimacy.

Stolen waters are sweet, and bread eaten in secret is pleasant. But he knows not that the dead are there; and that her guests are in the depths of hell (Proverbs, 9: 17,18).

Who can find a virtuous woman? Her price is far above rubies. The heart of her husband doth safely trust in her, so that he shall have no need of spoil (Proverbs, chapter 31: 10,11).

SEX—THE GIFT OF WOUNDING AND HEALING

Sex is one of the most complex aspects of a person's life. Perhaps, no other area of life holds similar mystery, charm, excitement; yet accompanied by so much potential for pain, destructive behavior, conflict, and tragedy. The Biblical quotations above point to the remarkable contrast involved in dealing with sex. It draws someone in by offering the pleasantries and it mesmerizes him/her by the promised excitement but it minimizes the potential for devastating consequences. The irresponsibility of our society regarding how to deal with sex is nothing less than alarming. One survey reports that over the past 20 years, opinion polls have been consistent in showing that about 35% of adults say that premarital sex is always or almost always wrong. Yet 95% of the respondents in the survey claimed to have had sex before marriage. (Quoted in a 2007 public health report that was written by Lawrence B. Finer.)

The overwhelming emphasis on sex as an end in itself or sex merely for pleasure defies commonsense considering the potential consequences. It should not surprise us then that the divorce rate is near 50%. Sex should come with responsibility. It should come with a significant aspect of marital relationship called intimacy. Sex on the fly is exciting but fleeting. Sex accompanied by a lasting intimate relationship is extremely satisfying. After all, that is what most women yearn for—an abiding trustworthy, loving, caring partner. Marriage relationships could become more stable if men would share that kind of bond with women.

PARADIGM 9: LAW OF DIMINISHING RETURNS

The paradigm for this topic uses the metaphor borrowed from economics to indicate that sex has an emotional component and the level of satisfaction decreases with the increasing amount of emotional input. (See *Paradigms of Marriage*, pp. 129-131.) Emotion, by its very nature, cannot be sustained indefinitely. Similarly, like the economic law of diminishing returns, sex waxes and wanes. Convinced otherwise by the flurry of images deceiving the public that those on the screen, magazines, or on the billboards enjoy sexual pleasures limitlessly, many seek this elusive passion in vain. Couples need to revise their concept of sex and invest instead in promoting intimacy. That's how the pleasure would endure. S. I. McMillen said it well:

> The love that is thoughtful and unselfish makes life's greatest dreams come to pass, but sex without love can make of life a horrible nightmare ("*The Superlatives of Sex*", *The Marriage Affair*, p.382).

There can be sex without intimacy and intimacy without sex but intimacy with sex is not merely a fleeting experience but it brings lasting satisfaction. It is possible to have fun without romance but it is almost impossible to have romance without fun.

PARADIGM 9 EXPLAINED

The Law of Diminishing Returns is a principle in economics that states:

> After a certain point, further increases in a particular factor of production lead to progressively smaller increases in output. The idea [is] that, after a certain point, more effort or investment in a project brings less reward or profit (*The Tormont Webster's Illustrated Encyclopedia Dictionary*).

The more one focuses on sex, the less he/she is likely to have lasting satisfaction: the more one focuses on sex with intimacy, the more likely he/she will achieve lasting satisfaction. The more one focuses on increasing sexual excitement, sexual activity, and even sexual deviancy, the more he/she experiences a declining level of sexual satisfaction and pleasure. Therefore, the more sexual activity is increased beyond the optimum point, the less the satisfaction. **Focusing on sex leads toward the pit: focusing on sexual intimacy leads toward paradise**. The best way to achieve the highest level of sexual satisfaction is within loving heterosexual marriage relationship.

SEX as a WEAPON

Some husbands and wives use sex as a weapon to punish their spouse. That is a double-edged sword. It is a sure way to attack the sacred bond between the partners. Because sex is an emotionally charged issue, withholding sex could inadvertently introduce another problem into the relationship. It could lead to hostility. Men gain intimacy through sex and respond to their wives with affection, which women need.

ISSUES AFFECTING SATIFYING SEX

Satisfying sex may be hampered by various means: anxiety, aging, ill health, tiredness, financial problems, illicit affairs, lack of affection between partners, fear of premature ejaculation, guilt, religious stereotype, fulfilling prophecy caused by fear of old age, and many other issues. Youth often see over age fifty to be a limit to sexual activity. When we reach fifty, we may well wonder: where in the world did we get that idea! After studying the subject, we discovered that sex gets better with age, providing the person is healthy. One informed writer ventured to say that a twenty-five-year-old would have difficulty competing with a healthy sixty-year-old. Statistics support that view.

Aging is a factor when illness occurs. Near age fifty or soon thereafter both men and women may be affected by drastic emotional and/or physiological changes in their body leading to menopause or burnout syndrome. Women may be affected by a drastic reduction in the estrogen hormone and men are more likely to suffer burnout syndrome, reduction in testosterone, and even prostate issues. The regular burden of life may also affect men and women. There is also the accumulation of years of poor eating habits, reduced sleep, and lessening of exercise. Dr. Eric Rimm, from Harvard University School of Public Health, told us that problem of erection in men may be a sign of impending heart attack. Fortunately, medical science has answers for most sexual issues that limit performance.

ALERT

Marriage therapists counsel us to be prepared for changes toward sex as aging occurs. Desire may not be as strong as in earlier years. It will not be business as usual. Caution must be taken less the couples end up drifting apart or divorced. *The Janus Report* revealed that there was no major difference in sexual frequency between twenty-five and over sixty-five-year-olds. Sexual response is a healthy part of marriage relationships and should not be denied because of age or spirituality. **Sex provides a unique means of maintaining the sacred bond between husband and wife at any age.**

KEY to PASSIONATE SEX

Most people today receive their feeling and knowledge—consciously or subconsciously, directly or indirectly---about sexual satisfaction from the prevailing fads in our immoral society. The movies, billboards, news, magazines, music etc. are filled with polluted images directed at us like a raging storm. Most people absorb it and even delight in having more and more of it. Let's be logical for a moment. How could meeting someone for the first time in one's life and kissing and having sex after a few minutes make any logical sense. But that is repeated over and over on the Hollywood screens. There is no loud protest. Our youth now think that it is normal. Many marriages are influenced by these images and, as expected, end in conflict and divorce.

The unavoidable key is found in the Bible. Marriage is between a man and a woman and sex between them is sacred. Love, true love, is the basis of the relationship. God condemns sex outside of the marriage relationship (See I Corinthians, chapter 6). The Bible also counsels couples not to deny their spouse of sexual relations unless there is consent between them. In other words, the apparent quest for spiritual purity does not permit one spouse to separate from his/her partner without consent. Sex in the relationship is a gift to help couples maintain intimacy.

Dr. Barbara DeAngelis described the key to sexual satisfaction by telling us that it takes one key for a woman to open a man's affection but it takes two keys for a man to open a woman's affection (See *Paradigms of Marriage*, pp.142-143). **This information is important.**

Activities

Paradigm 9: Sex & Intimacy

Read the chapter on Sex & Intimacy then answer the questions which follow.

1. What is your definition of "intimacy?" Write your thoughts:

   _____

   _____

   _____

   _____

2. What is your opinion of sex without intimacy? You do not have to write <u>your</u> personal story.

   _____

   _____

   _____

   _____

3. Write True or False for each statement-T for true and F for false.

   a) _____ Sex and intimacy are not the same.

   b) _____ Sex for physical pleasure is just as meaningful as sex in a successful marital relationship.

   c) _____ It is all right to have sex outside of marriage if it is more pleasurable with someone else.

   d) _____ Some males between 40 and 70 years of age may have arousal difficulties.

   e) _____ About 48 percent of women may have difficulty getting excited about sex.

   f) _____ Many women may still be in the arousal stage long after their husbands have already had orgasm.

   g) _____ According to some therapists, sexual unhappiness is widespread.

   h) _____ Sex is an area of potential conflict.

4. In your marriage relationship, what is your attitude towards sex? Write your own thoughts. Choose a relaxing 30 minutes to dialogue with your spouse.

   _____

   _____

   _____

   _____

5. Complete these statements:

   ➤ I deny my spouse sex when…

   _____

   _____

   _____

   _____

➤ I have hidden fears about sex because…

_____

_____

_____

_____

➤ I discuss my concerns with my spouse/partner and I am relieved when he/she is…

_____

_____

_____

_____

6. Write "F" for fact and "O" for opinion after each statement:
   a) _____ Many sexual problems in marriage are caused by tension and unhappiness.
   b) _____ During the declining years, arousals may take longer because the body is responding slower.
   c) _____ Divorce may result if, as couples grow older, adjustments are not made to cope with the changes which occur.
   d) _____ When couples grow older, they don't need sex.
   e) _____ Men have more of the testosterone hormone than women.
   f) _____ Testosterone in men creates a demand for sexual expression every few days.
   g) _____ There is a direct relationship between sex and health.
   h) _____ Tiredness can alter your ability to perform fully to the satisfaction of your spouse.
   i) _____ Many people are unable to perform sexually when under stress.
   j) _____ Sex with your partner is not truly great and lasting without intimacy.
   k) _____ It is best to have an intimate dialogue after a conflict to resolve the problem before engaging in sex.
   l) _____ There is an emotional advantage to couples when engaging in "make-up sex".
   m) _____ Many married couples could be happier together if they realized how men and women are different.

7. Read Dr. Steve and Cathy Broody's counsel on page 135 in *Paradigms of Marriage* and write your response. Share your response with your spouse.

_____

_____

_____

_____

8. How can you as a spouse deal with problems that affect a healthy sexual relationship? Write your personal view.

_____

_____

_____

_____

9. List some of the issues you have with sex and intimacy in your marriage and discuss these with your spouse. Pick two issues from your list and brainstorm with your spouse. Write the ideas you both have come up with to make the situation better and work on them. Enter your successes/failures in a daily journal and dialogue at least once each week on how you can turn each failure into a success.

    Issues: _____
    _____
    _____
    _____
    _____
    _____

    Pick two issues—brainstorm:

    _____
    _____
    _____
    _____

10. Write your responses to the comments in the boxes on page 131 in *Paradigms of Marriage.*

    _____
    _____
    _____
    _____

11. Take turns relating to your spouse about an uncomfortable personal episode that might have caused you to disengage from sexual relationship with him/her and that you feel may occur again. Discuss the problem and suggest ways to avoid its future occurrence. Take notes as you do this activity.

    _____
    _____
    _____
    _____

12. Read pages 144 and 145 in *Paradigms of Marriage,* then write your answer to the question: What can your spouse do to increase your desire for intimacy and a fulfilling sexual relationship? Discuss the details with each other and record your ideas.

    _____
    _____
    _____
    _____

Chapter Ten: Spirituality

Paradigm Ten: God's Design
(*Paradigms of marriage*, pages 148-170)

Men fill the role of leadership: Women possess the power of influence.
Ignoring the differences leads to the PIT, accepting and fostering them lead to PARADISE.

> For this cause shall a man leave his father and mother, and shall be joined unto his
> wife, and they two shall be one flesh (Gen. 2: 24).

CONNECTION

See if these episodes between two couples remind you of the value of intimacy in marriage relationships.

1. A wife and her husband were experiencing a period of lowered feeling of closeness. He tried to put his newly discovered marital strategies to work in order to get that full feeling flowing again. Then it happened. They were sitting peacefully in the living room. Then he began connecting with his wife through conversation. Nothing specific was driving the exchange. However, it drifted into talking about himself. He described how he was feeling and proceeded to analyze it in some detail, describing any issues that came to mind. She began to quiz him curiously about the issues he raised. Then she made a comment that surprised him a bit. His wife expressed that she was so pleased that he opened up and talked to her about himself in so much detail. From that moment, they connected in a way that left him feeling that, after many years of marriage, they were still growing toward an even deeper relationship.

2. Another couple was seeking ways to enhance their relationship after about four years of marriage, but issue after issue arose that challenged them. Both were in their second marriage experience, one caused by divorce and the other by death. The husband was in the public library engaged in writing when he thought of calling his wife just for contact. She began to express how she loved him and thanked him for caring for her and paying attention to her concerns. Taken by surprise, he thought to himself that she was not only expressing her gratitude but her love. They both thanked God for His favor toward them.

GOD'S PURPOSE

The foregoing episodes should remind us of what God expects from married couples. Our Creator pointed out that the purpose of marriage is to bring a woman and a man into a permanent bond—a "one flesh" experience. We may follow society and denigrate marriage, engage in premarital sex, disrespect our spouse by committing adultery, participate in aberrant activities, and perpetuate conflicts, all of which lead to pain and problems. Or, we may follow God's counsels regarding honoring the marriage relationship and enjoy peace and pleasure.

Couples may increase their intimacy when they choose to share in spiritual activities and participate in projects to help others. Some people consider sex as the way to achieve closeness but that view is far too limited. Maintaining openness with each other and seizing opportunities to share in meaningful activities certainly offer couples another satisfying way to intimacy. Seeking every opportunity to satisfy your spouse's need should be borne in mind and practiced regularly. Then use love language to tell each other how much you appreciate him/her. Do not take for granted that your spouse should know you care. Verbalize it! Doing so brings your feeling to life and makes a significant impact on your spouse.

In 1 Peter chapter 3, the Bible offers couples wise counsels. The husband should live considerately with his wife, bestow honor on her, learn successful strategies to woo her or else his salvation may be in jeopardy. God expects him to provide wise leadership. The wife should be supportive of her husband, develop her inner qualities, and employ her unique gift of influence in dealing with her husband and children. Both are "heirs together for the grace of life".

GOD'S DIVINE DESIGN

In the first chapter of the Bible, God revealed that He created a man and a woman in His own image:

> So God created man in His own image, in the image of God created He him; male and female create He them. And God blessed them, and God said unto them. Be fruitful, and multiply, and replenish the earth, and subdue it: and have dominion--- over every living thing that moves upon the earth (Genesis, 1: 27,28).

The final chapter of the Old Testament mentions marriage/family; the first chapter of the New Testament mentions marriage/family, and the final chapter of the Bible mentions marriage/family. Should not any well thinking person consider that marriage and family are important to God? We do not need to guess because God has made it clear:

> And you shall love the Lord your God with all your heart, and with all your soul, and with all your might. And these words, which I command you this day, shall be in your heart. And you shall teach them diligently unto your children, and shall talk of them when you sit in your house, and when you walk by the way, and when you lie down, and when you rise up. And you shall bind them for a sign upon your hand, and they shall be as frontlets between your eyes. And you shall write them upon the posts of your house, and on your gates (Deuteronomy, 6: 5-9).

Now dear reader, when last have you seen or heard about this command given by the Almighty God who created us? Does this declaration not tell us precisely the purpose of the family? God designed the family, gave clear instructions on how it should function, and who is in charge and directly responsible to Him. He declared that the parents have a divine responsibility to present to their children constantly—not occasionally---who God is as presented in the first part of the quotation above. Any parent who fails to do so must answer to God. By fulfilling this responsibility, parents would insulate their children against any contrary influence that may assail them in public discourse, such as the Theory of Evolution that denies God's creatorship and ownership of this world, society's pressure for everyone, even children, to have sex outside of marriage, and the government of Western countries enforcing laws to destroy families, namely, abortion on demand, encouraging single families, and homosexual relationships.

The purpose of marriage and the family is to perpetuate the name of God on the earth. Anyone who attempts to corrupt God's original plan by diverting from God's design for marriage must answer to God Himself. By definition, marriage can only be between a man and a woman. Any other relationship cannot be Biblical marriage.

No man-made reasoning can circumvent the declaration in Ephesians, 5: 23. Paul likens the marriage relationship to God and the Church. The function of the man and woman in the home must pattern the divine relationship of Christ and His church, that is referred to as his bride. Do we have the authority to change God's divinely designated order? We would do so at the risk of offending God and receiving the wrath of His fiery judgment.

Everything God does, He has a reason. Often, we cannot understand His purpose. Our task is to obey God's command until His purpose is revealed to us. He made clear in His word that sex is the sacred gift to bind a man and a woman together in a marriage relationship. Although we are tempted to change it into any other form, we risk God's displeasure. Let me make it clear: **I believe every one has the right to form any relationship he/she chooses. God has given all of us that freedom**. My comments are based only on what the Bible says and I choose to follow its guidance in my life.

PARADIGM 10: EGALITARIAN RELATIONSHIP

God has endowed man and woman with certain capabilities—spiritual, physical, mental, emotional, social. He equipped the man to be the leader and protector of the family. Only in cases where father is absent or unable should a woman assume leadership. Paradigm 10 explains clearly that **the married partners are equal but with different functions**. God has endowed women with gifts that men cannot equal. The key gift given to women is influence. This gift equips women to match men's strength and gift of leadership. Unfortunately, the commercial world and immoral women have corrupted this gift. Christian women may still use it gracefully in their home and elsewhere to obtain their desire, a peaceful and loving relationship. This does not mean that women should not pursue their goals and accomplishments. They should take into serious consideration how God designed the family and the best way to achieve lasting success.

RADICAL CHANGE: WOMEN'S MOVEMENT

When Elizabeth Cady Stanton led a team of women to what may be considered the nascence of the women's movement at the first women's convention on July 19,20, 1848, she may not have envisioned what the women's movement would become. Her list of grievances did not envision women's abortion rights, surrogate motherhood, unisex bathrooms, women serving in military combat, homosexual rights, and so on. Neither do I think she was seeking equality with men at the peril of abandoning raising socially responsible children and abandoning the homemaking to her husband. Let us take a look at what these women were agitating for:

- Married women were legally dead in the eyes of the law
- Women were not allowed to vote
- Women had to submit to laws when they had no voice in their formation
- Married women had no property rights
- Husbands had legal power over and responsibility for their wives to the extent that they could imprison or beat them with impunity
- Divorce and child custody laws favored men, giving no rights to women
- Women had to pay property taxes although they had no representation in the levying of these taxes
- Most occupations were closed to women and when women did work they were paid only a fraction of what men earned
- Women were not allowed to enter professions such as medicine or law
- Women had no means to gain an education since no college or university would accept women students
- With only a few exceptions, women were not allowed to participate in the affairs of the church
- Women were robbed of their self-confidence and self-respect, and were made totally dependent on men

Historically women have suffered tragically at the hands of cruel men and unjust laws. They had to cry out and surely the God of heaven certainly heard them. Jesus demonstrated his concern for women when he walked the earth. Contemporary men should follow His example to love, honor, support, and care for women. Men should encourage women to excel in their God-given talents.

A supporter of the women's cause, Frederick Douglas, the black orator and activist, spoke in their convention supporting women's suffrage, the most difficult of the twelve demands. It was voted but it was the only one that did not receive a unanimous approval. This "Decaration of Sentiments" passed at the first women's convention launched a tedious revolutionary campaign that still has repercusions today.

What is known as the second wave of the women's movement was launched in the 1960s and it had a twist that was, rightly or wrongly, interpreted to be women's independence from men. Consequently, for the succeeding decades, men have been struggling to know how to deal with women to avoid ridicule and how to interpret a father/husband's place in the home. It became worse when women began to earn more then their husbands and money gained a new source of power. During the 1960s and 1970s, some women assumed the role of agitating to catapult women to leadership positions that place them in ascendency over men. During the process, they promoted the idea of abolishing the distinction between the sexes. The idea of easing women from under the burden of subservience in which they were placed in previous generations became an inadequate quest. Prior to this, women strived for parity in an egalitarian social system. Now it seemed women needed not only being equal to men but striving for a superiority or rulership over men.

Even if the women did not intend to seek for ascendency, that is how men perceived their quest. At least, some women were vocal about not needing men. A spirit of unhealthy rivalry began that bore bitter fruits. Lesbian and homosexual practices were encouraged and marriages started to crumble as women paid less attention to homemaking, considering it to be meanial and domestic.

CONSIDER THIS

The attitude of some women advocates was to thow out the "baby with the bathwater". (An appropriate pun.) How different it would be if women would use their God-given gift of influence to mold society into wholesome moral functioning. God gave women the amazing gift of childbearing with the amazing capacity for childrearing. **God endowed women with certain graces: tenderness, patience, caring, nurturing, capacity to love deeply, keen sense of impending danger, intuition, gracefulness, charm, and influence.** Abandoning that critical role in their quest for fame, wealth, and power, many modern women assign the upbringing of their children to a Godless immoral society. Most of the children in our modern societies are now tragically destitute of the powerful positive influence only mothers can provide. Often, they neither have the time nor do they consider it a critical need.

Today our society is destroyed because children lack proper upbringing and moral compass while their mothers are preoccupied with climbing the ladder in society and gaining power, fame, wealth, and prestige that they consider to be more noble goals. Unfortunately, even Christian women are caught in this web of women seeking temporal power and success. I would assume that the saying "the hand that rocks the cradle rules the world" does not mean the home but halls of parliament and/or the commercial world. A woman is no longer revered for the quality of her family but her worldly accomplishments. Children and homelife become appendages.

Do you still wonder why our society is overcome by unchecked violence, social drugs, and unspeakable immoral conduct? Are you still amazed by the alarming eighty to ninety percent broken homes? Is there need of research to determine the reason for political leaders, so called role models, and even clergymen to abandon morality and seek passionately their god of unlimited wealth, public recognition, political power, social prestige, and sexual perversions?

God endowed women with certain built-in gifts that men cannot match. Desiring to expose women's innate differences from men, John Gray published a book that describes women as coming from Venus, a completely different planet from men. God equipped men with abilities to provide and protect their family and society: women are specially endowed with the gift of complementing, nurturing, inspiring, and loving. Drunk with the wine of womens's ascendency over men in our enlightened society, even some men are becoming passionate about women abandoning their gifts and claiming more noble achievements than a successful family. That is too domestic! Let the babysitters, daycares, husbands, social media, and McDonald's restaurants care for such mundane matters. When the children become monsters and prey on the society, we will see what we can do to help. Of course, once society dismissed God and the Bible, we are all left to our own uncontrolled devices anyhow.

APPEAL To WOMEN

Women, especially Christian women, need to develop their God-given talents to the highest level possible. But they should remember the source of true happiness and their divine purpose in this world. To raise morally upright children, cherish a loving socially sensitive husband, and foster a Christian family should still be a coveted prize for wise women. Can Christian women stop long enough in their quest for achievement and independence to listen to the counsel from the wisest person who ever lived:

> Who can find a virtuous woman? For her price is far above rubies. The heart of her husband safely trusts in her, so that he shall have no need of spoil (Proverbs, 31: 10-11).

When women return to their true calling of raising honorable, praiseworthy families, the men may likely return to take their rightful place in a loving home, previously considered a place of refuge, a sanctuary. Then will marriage fulfill its purpose.

SINGLE WOMEN: This workbook and *Paradigms of Marriage* deal with marriage. It does not attempt to deal with single women. That subject is dealt with cursorily in the Drs. Robert & Pamela Samms' book *Family & Faith*.

PERSONAL STORY

After what is said in the previous section, you may think we don't want women to be educated but stay at home to cook, wash, and clean. WRONG!

This year is Robert's fiftieth year as a minister of the gospel and fifty-second year of marriage to two women, consecutively of course. Robert's first wife, Pamela, was his sweetheart for five years before they married in 1964. They attended the same boarding high school, sat in the same classes, and graduated together. They attended college together and left to get married while they were financially broke students. He still remembers that they spent all but a few dollars of their money to pay for the wedding on the Andrews University campus in Michigan. They ate sandwiches for most of their honeymoon and had to borrow one hundred dollars from a friend so they could leave the Four Flags hotel in Niles, Michigan, to travel by bus to a sales job in Edmonton, Alberta.

Pam did not complete her secondary education degree and Robert had just completed his Bachelor of Theology degree. He pledged to her that he would help her complete her degree and support her in the career she chose. After working in sales for a few months in Alberta, Robert accepted an appointment as principal of Grand Bahama Academy, a private elementary and middle school in the Bahamas. Pam taught at the school until their first son was born. Two years later, three months after their first daughter was born, they left for Andrews University, where Pam registered to complete her degree. Not wanting her to be unduly distracted, they hired a live-in helper to assist with domestic chores. To provide funds, Robert worked over thirty hours per week in two jobs while taking full class load for his master's degree.

During the following years, Pam attended three other universities (McGill University, University of Alberta, and Argosy University). After acquiring several diplomas, Pam achieved her EdD in differentiated learning. She taught for over forty years in four countries and conducted seminars for teachers before passing away in 2012. They grew up four Christian children-two boys and two girls-who are making significant contributions to society. They are married and committed to bringing up their twelve children as responsible Christian citizens. **Richard, Tamaylia, Royland, and Sherine learned from their mother that, despite her academic and professional excellence, being a devoted Christian wife and mother and raising her loving family successfully were her crowning life's achievements**. They are now patterning her model with their families.

Robert's current wife, Petula, could testify that he has given her every support to advance her education and develop her career. Petula (Precious) teams with him in a Marriage/Family Education Ministry as a certified marriage facilitator. Petula brings a valuable set of skills to their marriage and ministry, that of successful single motherhood. After only a few years of marriage, her former husband left her with an infant daughter. She suspended her education to stay home and raise her daughter. Petula is using her experience gained in that process to help other women who are facing similar circumstances. During her hiatus to raise her child, Petula used her musical skills to contribute significantly to the music of her church in Montreal.

Petula and Pamela never confused their role as confident woman and competent wife and mother. Women can balance their career and family successfully and when they conflict, family should take precedence.

Robert shared the home duties with Pamela and Petula as needed but he surrendered leadership of the home responsibilities to his wife and she conceded leadership of the family to him. Adjustments were/are made as needed and in both relationships the result was/is harmonious functioning together. His wife decides the furniture, colors, decoration of the home, the meal program and even who may be invited to the home. Over the years Robert would cook and wash the dishes when needed but he considered it his duty to take care of the building and yard. Budgets are planned together but he handles the financial negotiations and keeps a constant eye on their finances. His wife has the last word on which house to purchase but Robert takes on the responsibility of negotiating and closing the deal. Robert concedes that some women do a better job handling the budget than men. Therefore, the specifics should be negotiated according to the ability and interest of each partner in the relationship.

All the children depended on their mother for motherly love and care. She was an example of distinguished womanhood for her daughters to emulate and sons to remember when choosing a wife. By objective standards, it could be concluded that all four children chose spouses that complement their character and upbringing. Both of their sons' wife held Pam in high regard and now offer their respect to Petula, who is an exemplary woman of faith and a loving wife to their dad. Robert sets the tone of spiritual and moral leadership in the home, provides guidance, and sets and maintains standards for the children to pattern.

Obviously, not all couples and situations can fit into one mold. Husbands and wives may accommodate each other in the day to day details but certain functions are best assigned according to roles. **In order to achieve harmony, partners should engage in constant peaceful negotiations, loving accommodations, and considerate adjustments.**

A BIBLICAL EXAMPLE FOR WOMEN

Consider how Abigail used her **gift of influence** when her husband acted foolishly. (See: I Samuel, chapter 25.) David was only a rival for leadership in Israel. He had only a small band of men and limited supplies. When David was angry with her husband because he despised David's request for food, Abigail called upon her intuition and unleashed her feminine graces that are truly unigue to women to influence David. He threatened to destroy their family when Abigail wisely intervened. God rewarded her richly by influencing David to respond kindly to her.

Through her amazing influence, Abigail caused David to spare her husband's life and her family. Later David married her and made her queen of the nation. Consider the impact she must have had in influencing King David's policies when she became queen.

SERVICE

There is special bond that can develop between a man and his wife (and children) when they work together to bless others. They enjoy shared meaning and purpose as they work toward a common goal. As they work together as a team, their reliance on each other grows and their support for each other is increased.

SPIRITUAL LIFE

Those persons who are committed to a Christian lifestyle have the advantage of following the life and teachings of Jesus, the Christ, and the principles enunciated in the Bible, God's inspired guide to every person. Even if someone does not believe in God, he/she would enjoy a significant advantage should he/she follow the moral guidance of Scripture and its counsels regarding marital and family relationships. Most of the principles relating to conducting a successful marriage that secular research has yielded may be found hidden in the pages of the Bible. Therefore, should couples yield themselves to Jesus, the Christ, before embarking on their marital journey, their path to marital "paradise" would more likely be assured. We highly recommend that you take Jesus, the Christ, as the Lord of your life and Counselor in your marriage and family relationships.

Activities

Paradigm 10: Spirituality and Service

Write short answers for the following questions:

1. Read page 153 in the *Paradigms of Marriage,* then explain your understanding of the role of leadership in the family as God designed it.

   _____

   _____

   _____

   _____

2. What, from a Biblical perspective, is your understanding of marriage?

   _____

   _____

   _____

   _____

3. From a Biblical standpoint, did God expect both man and woman to perform the same function in marriage or exchange roles? Explain.

   _____

   _____

   _____

   _____

4. Using Peter's counsel on pages 164 and 165 in *Paradigms of Marriage,* indicate your answers by placing a check mark beside the statements of beliefs you practice. Validate your answers by checking in with each other.

<u>Men</u>

Statements Often Sometimes Not at all

I live with consideration for my wife.			
I believe in sharing my life with my wife.			
My spiritual growth shows in how I treat my wife.			

<u>Women</u>

Statements Often Sometimes Not at all

I use grace and my influence to win over my husband.			
I am a supportive wife to my husband.			
I let go of grudges or malice against my husband.			

5. List 3 things you believe to be your admirable qualities as a wife or husband. Discuss these with your spouse and decide whether there are other positive traits you would like each other to cultivate and for what reason(s).

_____

_____

_____

_____

6. What Biblical proof do you have that "God invented sex"? Write your findings and matching texts.

_____

_____

_____

_____

Read pages 160 and 161 in *Paradigms of Marriage*. Describe briefly in point form what God requires of you regarding love. Discuss your findings with your partner/spouse and list the ideals. Dialogue about it and, together, come to an understanding of how you can support each other in reaching those ideals.

What God requires (the ideals):

_____

_____

_____

_____

Ways to support each other in reaching those ideals:

_____

_____

_____

_____

7. Describe your Biblical role as a wife/husband and discuss the findings with your partner/ spouse. Discuss how you can both strive for reaching the ideals. Record verses from the Bible that you have used as Scriptural evidence.

_____

_____

_____

_____

8. What is your concept of "service"? Explain.

_____

_____

_____

_____

```MY MARRIAGE GROWTH COVENANT

By God's grace, I pledge to use the principles I have learned from *Paradigms of Marriage* to enhance and grow my relationship with my spouse.
I pledge to use my personal choice option to discover what I can do to enhance the happiness of my spouse and improve our marriage, rather than focusing on my spouse's attitude toward me.
I pledge to be more sensitive to my spouse by sorting out our ten needs of nature and nurture and men's needs/women's needs. I will endeavor to use the strategies of negotiation and accommodation to fulfill them.
I pledge to avoid the ten negative attitudes that lead a marriage toward the pit and I will endeavor to implement the ten positive attributes that will lead our marriage toward happiness and success.
I pledge to adopt a financial family plan that will assist us to achieve and maintain freedom from unsecured debt.
I pledge to accept the Biblical principles relating to marriage and intimacy:
I will use them constantly to undergird our relationship.

I prayerfully and sincerely petition God's grace to assist me in fulfilling my role as a loving and caring spouse and, thereby, achieving a happy and successful marriage.

Signed:_____Date:_____
       Spouse Making the Covenant
Signed:_____Date_____
       Spouse/partner as Witness
Signed:_____Date:_____
       Ms. Petula Samms, Marriage Facilitator
Signed: _____Date: _____
       Dr. Robert O. Samms, Marriage Educator

Answers to Questions in Each Chapter

<u>Paradigm 1</u>
<u>True and False Questions</u>
- a) True
- b) True
- c) True
- d) False
- e) False
- f) True
- g) False
- h) True
- i) True
- j) False
- k) True

<u>Paradigm 2</u>
<u>True and False Questions</u>
- a) True
- b) True
- c) True
- d) True
- e) True
- f) False
- g) True
- h) True
- i) True
- j) False

<u>Paradigm 4</u>
<u>True and False Questions</u>
- a) True
- b) True
- c) True
- d) True
- e) False

f) False

g) True

h) True

i) True

j) False

Paradigm 5
True and False Questions

a) True

b) True

c) True

d) True

e) True

f) False

g) True

h) True

i) True

j) False

k) True

Paradigm 7
Fact/Opinion Questions

a) Fact

b) Fact

c) Fact

d) Fact

e) Fact

f) Fact

g) Opinion

h) Opinion

Paradigm 9
True/False Questions

a) True

b) False

c) False

d) True

e) True

f) True

g) True

h) True

Paradigm 9
Fact/Opinion Questions

    a) Fact

    b) Fact

    c) Fact

    d) Opinion

    e) Fact

    f) Fact

    g) Fact

    h) Fact

    i) Fact

    j) Fact

    k) Fact

    l) Fact

    m) Fact

Bibliography

BOOKS

Betcher, William and McCauley, Robie, *The Seven Basic Quarrels of Marriage*, New York: Villard Books, 1990.

DeAngelis, Barbara, *What Women Want Men to Know*, New York: Hyperion, 2001.

Dobson, James, *Marriage and Family*, Wheaton, Illinois: Tyndale Publishing, 2000.

Doyle, Laura, *The Surrendered Wife*, New York: Simon & Schuster, 2001.

Eldridge, John, *You Have What It Takes*, Nashville: Nelson Books, 2004.

Glasser, William and Carleen, *Getting Together and Staying Together*, New York: HarperCollins, 2000.

Gottman, John, *Why Marriages Succeed or Fail?* New York: Simon & Schuster, 1994

Janus, Samuel S. and Cynthia, *The Janus Report*, New York: John Wiley & Sons, 1993

Lerner, Harriett, *The Dance of Anger*, New York: HarperCollins, 1997.

Mace, David, *Close Companions*, North Carolina: The Marriage Enrichment Handbook, 1982.

Ramsay, Dave, *Financial Peace*, New York: Viking Penguin Books, 1995.

Samms, Robert and Pamela, *Family & Faith*, Bloomington, IN.: iUniverse Publishing, 2011.

Samms, Robert, *Making Marriage Meaningful*, Lincoln, NE.: iUniverse Publishing, 2005.

Samms, Robert, *Paradigms of Marriage*, Lincoln, NE: iUniverse Publishing, 2006.

Schnarch, David, *Passionate Marriage*, New York: Henry Holt & Co., 1997

Van Pelt, Nancy, *Train Up A Child*, Hagerstown, MD.: Review and Herald Publishing, 1984.

REFERENCE & ARTICLES

Anna Miller, "Can This Marriage Be Saved?", posted March 7, 2017

Beth Kotz, Unique Financial Challenges That Arise in A 2nd Marriage, posted February 27, 2017

Bible, King James Version

Bible, Revised Standard Version

Johns Hopkins Research, Released July 13, 2016

The Tormont Webster's Illustrated Encyclopedia Dictionary, Montreal: Tormont Publications, 1990.

Website: BetterMarriages.Org

Printed in the United States
By Bookmasters